קַבָּלַת שַׁבָּת

THE SABBATH EVENING SERVICE

קַבָּלַת שַׁבָּת

THE
SABBATH
EVENING
SERVICE

with a new
translation and
commentary by
CHAIM RAPHAEL

BEHRMAN HOUSE, INC.   PUBLISHERS   NEW YORK

ACKNOWLEDGMENTS

The author and publisher thank the following for permission to reprint:

"The Request," by Solomon ibn Gabirol, and excerpts from "Lord, Where Shall I Find You?" by Judah Halevi, from *The Penguin Book of Hebrew Verse*, edited and translated by T. Carmi. Copyright © 1985 by T. Carmi. Reprinted by permission of Penguin Books, Ltd.

Library of Congress Cataloging-in-Publication Data
Arvit (Sabbath). English & Hebrew.
   The Sabbath evening service : with a new
translation and commentary = [Kabalat Shabat]
   Prayers in English and Hebrew; commentary in English.
   1. Sabbath—Liturgy—Texts. 2. Siddurim—Texts.
3. Judaism—Liturgy—Texts. 4. Arvit (Sabbath)
I. Raphael, Chaim. II. Title. III. Title:
Kabalat Shabat.
BM675.S3Z5567   1985   296.4'1   85-19180
ISBN 0-87441-418-0

Cover/Book Design by Robert J. O'Dell

Cover Photograph by Marshall Henricks
Window at Temple Ohabei Shalom, Brookline, Massachusetts
Design concept by Rabbi Albert Goldstein

Published by Behrman House, Inc., 1261 Broadway, New York,
N.Y. 10001
Manufactured in the United States of America

CONTENTS

FOR THE WORSHIPER

When Jews come together in the synagogue on Friday evening to welcome the Sabbath, it is a solemn—and happy—act of unification with their history and faith. What role do the prayers of the service play in this? In one sense, they are all-important: because they are old and hallowed, they are ready as a vehicle for what we feel. In another sense, the recital of prayers is less important than one's presence in the synagogue. Even if one sat silent, filled with the message of kinship that the Sabbath expresses, one would be receiving its blessing.

One can talk of the Sabbath's blessing in utilitarian terms. It is good to rest from one's weekly work, to forget the cares of the workaday world. It is a marvel that this idea came into the world through the first section of the Jewish Bible—the Torah.

But to see it only in these terms would be to ignore the profound meaning that the Sabbath has had for Jews throughout their long history. To Jews, the Sabbath is not a rest from life but a reaffirmation of what life is about. One does not want to be left with the sense of futility expressed in T. S. Eliot's verse: *I have known the evenings, mornings, afternoons / I have measured out my life with coffee spoons.*

One breaks away from this in reaching out, on Shabbat Eve, to deeper forms of experience. One can experience these moments in many settings—in listening to great music, in literature that moves us, or in the encounter with love or death. The trivia fall away before a perception that includes magic; and this kind of magic is manifest in the celebration of Shabbat. One may feel it at the synagogue or at home, in the friendship of communal prayer or in the light of the Shabbat candles sparkling on our dinner tables.

In these and other forms, we seek to affirm the meaning of Jewish existence. The story is too stirring to touch us only from the outside; it affects us in the deepest core of our being. We cannot always put this feeling into words, but it surfaces in the affirmation of the *Sh'ma* or in the happiness of singing together the familiar *zemirah Shalom aleichem.*

This personal feeling can arise spontaneously as we listen to an ancient prayer or hear the words of a psalm. But the meaning can be even deeper if ideas are opened up, as we read, through comments on the text before us, drawn from the richness of the Jewish tradition. A special feature of this prayerbook, therefore, is that it offers a running commentary, not to swamp the prayers with additional material but to be quietly available in the background.

As the users of this prayerbook will see, there is no rigid form for the commentary. Sometimes a new section of the service seems to call for a special introduction; but for the most part the comments start with a word, or a phrase, or an idea in a prayer or a psalm, and set out briefly to deepen the meaning. One may went to highlight the devotional significance of the particular word or phrase, but equally one may be called on to deal with history or myth, since there are no rigid boundaries to the faith that has come down to us and which we celebrate through this service of prayer.

At some points in the service we are listeners; at others, we speak or respond. In both, our personal feelings are stirred and the commentary will, I hope, deepen this feeling by opening up fresh avenues of thought.

Over a period of years, while this project was in my mind, I had the good fortune to discuss its approach and contents with a number of friends much more expert in the field than I am, and whose advice was therefore most valuable to me. Among them I would particularly like to thank (in alphabetical order) Rabbi Bernard J. Bamberger, Rabbi Miles Cohen, Rabbi Martin Freedman, Rabbi and Mrs. Emanuel Green, Rabbi Stephan O. Parnes, Rabbi Lee J. Paskind, and Rabbi Mordecai Waxman. I learned from them all, though they bear no responsibility, of course, for what finally appears here.

May I wish all who use this book: *Shabbat Shalom.*

Chaim Raphael

PUBLISHER'S NOTE

The service contained in this prayerbook may be used for worship on ordinary Sabbaths and those Sabbaths coinciding with Rosh Hodesh. It does not, however, include the liturgical variants required for a Sabbath that coincides with a Festival, Hol Hamoed, the Ten Days of Penitence, or Hanukkah.

סֵדֶר הַתְּפִלּוֹת
THE
ORDER OF
PRAYER

It is an old custom, on entering the
synagogue, to read these Bible verses silently as
one waits for the formal service to begin.
The familiar words offer a happy bridge from the
bustle of the week to the calm of Shabbat.

MAH TOVU

מַה־טֹּבוּ

מַה־טֹּבוּ אֹהָלֶיךָ, יַעֲקֹב,	1	How goodly are your tents, O Jacob,
מִשְׁכְּנֹתֶיךָ, יִשְׂרָאֵל.	2	your dwelling places, O Israel.

SILENT WORSHIP AND COMMUNAL PRAYER: Traditionally, *Mah Tovu* is a silent meditation. When we enter the synagogue, each of us is alone, as an individual, with God. Yet in coming together with our fellow Jews, we know that we are *not* alone. We have come here as part of the community of Israel. We are praying to God as a people.

WORDS OF THE MEDITATION: The first sentence (*Mah Tovu*) is from a very ancient poem in the Bible—perhaps from the time of the Exodus itself—known as "Balaam's blessing"; the other verses, as we shall see, are from the Psalms.

BALAAM'S BLESSING: In the Bible story (Numbers 22–24), the King of Moab hires a soothsayer called Balaam to curse the Jews, since, in being led by Moses to the Promised Land, they are about to cross his territory. But when Balaam tries, the curse cannot pass his lips. Instead, he finds himself blessing the Jews in a rhapsodic vision of the future:

How goodly are your tents, O Jacob, your dwelling places, O Israel.
Like palm groves that stretch out, like gardens beside a river,
Like aloes planted by the Lord, like cedars beside the water . . .

AGE OF THE BIBLE TEXT: William Foxwell Albright, the Christian scholar who strongly defended the authenticity of the Bible text, wrote of the Balaam Oracles: "To judge from the text of the Oracles, which were probably delivered, at least in part, by Balaam and remembered by word of mouth, Balaam was for some time a convert to Israel's faith during Moses's later life in Transjordan, and this temporary conversion is reflected in the content of the Oracles. . . . The evidence of style and grammar points to a date between the Song of Moses (Exodus 15) and the time of David (11th century B.C.E.)."

1 מַה־טֹבוּ אֹהָלֶיךָ, יַעֲקֹב — HOW GOODLY ARE YOUR TENTS, O JACOB: This ancient Bible verse (Numbers 24:5) has become, through history, a perfect evocation of the blessing that has flowed to Jews through the comfort and inspiration of gathering together regularly for prayer. It is very usual—almost universal—to find the words inscribed over the entrance porch to the synagogue.

2 מִשְׁכְּנֹתֶיךָ, יִשְׂרָאֵל — YOUR DWELLING PLACES, O ISRAEL: In Hebrew, the word *mishkan* ("dwelling place") means much more than a hall or meeting place. It is God's dwelling place. From the same Hebrew root (שכן), we get the word *shechinah* ("the Divine Presence"). The *mishkan* ("Tabernacle") that the ancient Hebrews carried with them in the wilderness was the focus of their faith.

וַאֲנִי בְּרֹב חַסְדְּךָ אָבוֹא בֵיתֶךָ, |1
אֶשְׁתַּחֲוֶה אֶל הֵיכַל קָדְשְׁךָ
בְּיִרְאָתֶךָ. |2
יְיָ אָהַבְתִּי מְעוֹן בֵּיתֶךָ, |3
וּמְקוֹם מִשְׁכַּן כְּבוֹדֶךָ.
וַאֲנִי אֶשְׁתַּחֲוֶה וְאֶכְרָעָה,
אֲבָרְכָה לִפְנֵי יְיָ עֹשִׂי. |4
וַאֲנִי תְפִלָּתִי לְךָ, יְיָ, עֵת רָצוֹן. |5
אֱלֹהִים, בְּרָב־חַסְדֶּךָ,
עֲנֵנִי בֶּאֱמֶת יִשְׁעֶךָ.

I come into Your House through
    the greatness of Your love.
I worship in Your holy Temple in
    reverence.
O Lord, I love the Presence in
    Your House,
the place where Your glory dwells.
I worship, and bow down, and bend
    the knee before God my Maker.
May my prayer come to You,
    O Lord, in a moment of grace.
O God, in the abundance of Your
    lovingkindness,
answer me in the truth of Your
    salvation.

חַסְדְּךָ — YOUR LOVE: This verse (Psalm 5:8) speaks of God's *ḥesed*, usually translated as "lovingkindness"; but the word "love" speaks to us more directly. 1

בְּיִרְאָתֶךָ — IN REVERENCE: The Hebrew word *yir'ah* means "fear," yielding "in fear of You" in most translations, but "reverence" for God is a deeper concept than fear of Him. 2

מְעוֹן בֵּיתֶךָ — THE PRESENCE IN YOUR HOUSE: The meaning of the Hebrew phrase becomes clear through the parallelism of this verse (Psalm 26:8). 3

אֲבָרְכָה — BEND THE KNEE: This sentence echoes the sense of worship evoked in Psalm 95:6 (p. 4). 4

וַאֲנִי תְפִלָּתִי לְךָ — MAY MY PRAYER COME TO YOU: This verse, which ends our private meditation, is from the sixty-ninth Psalm (v. 14). In Hebrew, the word for "prayer" (*tefillah*) conveys intense inner devotion, as in the formal *Tefillah* (*Amidah*), which is found later in the service. The whole of Psalm 69 is intensely personal in feeling. The poet who composed it reached deep down into human anguish to find strength in faith. The opening words of the psalm set the tone: 5

    Save me, O God, for the waters have engulfed me.
    I am sunk in deep mire and find no foothold. . . .
    I am weary with calling; my throat is dry;
    my eyes fail while I wait for God.

But his faith is restored in words with a double meaning for us today:

    For God will save Zion and will build the cities of Judah. . . .
    The offering of His servants shall possess it;
    those who cherish His name shall dwell there.

The Psalms, 150 in number, are drawn on in
every Jewish service—in the synagogue, in private worship,
and on all occasions, sad and joyous, of Jewish life.
The titles on many psalms show that they were designed
especially to celebrate Shabbat.

KABBALAT SHABBAT

קַבָּלַת שַׁבָּת

THE PSALM SEQUENCE: Tradition has brought together a sequence of psalms (starting on the next page) which are well attuned to the mood of our Shabbat service. In all, there are seven, which are thought to stand for the seven days of the week. A sequence of six, close together in the book of Psalms, is interrupted by a joyous interlude in which the favorite Psalm 29 is recited, as a prelude to our singing of *Lechah Dodi*.

THE POWER OF THE PSALMS: It is almost incredible that the psalms, which have such power to move us today, were composed at least 2,500 years ago, and in some cases as long ago as 3,000 years, in the days of King David. They continue to reach us at two distinct levels—as a people and as individuals.

GOD AND HIS PEOPLE: When the psalms were sung by the Levites in the Temple, the assembled multitudes heard their history coming to life: the God who loved His people was the Lord of Creation. The Jews had found the way to worship this God, which set them apart; but He was always the God—and Ruler—of all the world. We hear this double message repeatedly, as in Psalm 98, which is part of this sequence (p. 12): "He has remembered His lovingkindness and faith to the House of Israel; the power of our God to save has been manifest to the ends of the earth."

GOD AND THE INDIVIDUAL: Side-by-side with the triumphant majesty of the psalms—"Let the earth ring out in song to God"—we hear with equal power the words of quiet comfort to each individual soul. Alone, in doubt or anguish, God's presence sustains us. The ideal that the psalmist puts before us is an individual who lives a life of simplicity and honesty, a person "who speaks the truth in his heart." Countless generations, Jews and non-Jews alike, have understood this message of the psalmist and drawn strength from it.

IMAGERY OF THE PSALMS: The language of the psalms alternates between words of quiet truth and torrents of imagery that sweep us along with their power. In Psalm 29 (p. 15), we hear the latter in the paean of praise to God in the force of Nature:

The voice of God thunders, the Lord over mighty waters.
The voice of the Lord is power, the voice of the Lord is majesty.
The voice of the Lord breaks cedars, the Lord shatters the cedars of Lebanon.

But the psalm ends with gentle words that are familiar and beloved in every act of worship among Jews:

The Lord will give strength to His people,
the Lord will bless His people with peace.

For centuries, it has been customary to introduce
the Shabbat Eve service with this sequence of six psalms
supplemented by Psalm 29. The six
are all nature psalms, expressing the beauty of the universe
that emerged in the six days of creation.

THE SIX PSALMS

יְמֵי הַמַּעֲשֶׂה

Psalm 95

לְכוּ נְרַנְּנָה לַיְיָ, 1
נָרִיעָה לְצוּר יִשְׁעֵנוּ. 2
נְקַדְּמָה פָנָיו בְּתוֹדָה, 3
בִּזְמִרוֹת נָרִיעַ לוֹ.
כִּי אֵל גָּדוֹל יְיָ, 4
וּמֶלֶךְ גָּדוֹל עַל־כָּל־אֱלֹהִים.
אֲשֶׁר בְּיָדוֹ מֶחְקְרֵי־אָרֶץ,
וְתוֹעֲפוֹת הָרִים לוֹ.
אֲשֶׁר לוֹ הַיָּם וְהוּא עָשָׂהוּ,
וְיַבֶּשֶׁת יָדָיו יָצָרוּ.
בֹּאוּ נִשְׁתַּחֲוֶה וְנִכְרָעָה,
נִבְרְכָה לִפְנֵי יְיָ עֹשֵׂנוּ.

Come, let us sing to the Lord; let us cry out in joy to the Rock, our Salvation.
Let us come into His Presence in thanksgiving; with psalms we call to Him.
For the Lord is Almighty, a Ruler high above idols.
The depths of the earth are in His hands; the mountain peaks are His too.
The sea is His, He made it; the dry land, He shaped it.
Come, let us bow down and bend the knee, let us kneel before the Lord our Maker.

לְכוּ נְרַנְּנָה — LET US SING: In Hebrew, the word *nerannenah* is onomatopoeic in origin, with a most joyous ring. It is much happier than the usual word for "sing." It really expresses: "Let us sing for joy." **1**

נָרִיעָה — LET US CRY OUT: Here, again, the Hebrew word *nari'ah* expresses joy, though in itself the root, *rua'*, conveys a signal of excitement, and is familiar to us as the name (*teru'ah*) given to one of the rousing tunes played by the *shofar* at the Rosh Hashanah service. The parallel sense of joy in both halves of this verse has an even stronger effect in Hebrew, where one enjoys the alliteration used by the psalmist for "sing" and "cry out"—*nerannenah, nari'ah*. As always, it is difficult to convey in translation the grace and euphony of the original Hebrew of the Bible, even if the meaning emerges clearly. **2**

פָּנָיו — HIS PRESENCE: In the Temple, where these words were sung, the worshipers had a vivid sense of God's Presence. The Hebrew phrase means literally: "Let us come before His face." The same word for "His face" (*panav*) appears in the priestly blessing: "May God lift up His face (*panav*) unto you." Both passages convey an overwhelming sense of grace and holiness. **3**

כִּי אֵל גָּדוֹל יְיָ — FOR THE LORD IS ALMIGHTY: In the simple word *gadol* ("great"), we hear the omnipotence of the Creator. The Master of the Universe is revered with special intensity on Shabbat Eve when we try to understand the full meaning of Creation. **4**

כִּי הוּא אֱלֹהֵינוּ וַאֲנַחְנוּ עַם מַרְעִיתוֹ וְצֹאן יָדוֹ,	1	He is our God; we are the people of His pasture, the flock of His hand.
הַיּוֹם אִם בְּקֹלוֹ תִשְׁמָעוּ.	2	Today! If only you would hear His voice.
אַל תַּקְשׁוּ לְבַבְכֶם כִּמְרִיבָה, כְּיוֹם מַסָּה בַּמִּדְבָּר.	3	Harden not your heart, as at Merivah, as in the day of Massah in the wilderness.

1   הוּא אֱלֹהֵינוּ — HE IS OUR GOD: It seems puzzling, sometimes, that the word *elohim* for "God," used in the Bible so frequently (more than 2,000 times), is in the plural. The singular form *el* is the oldest Semitic word for God. It is seldom used in the Bible as the personal name of God, but almost always as an appellative. The Bible scholar Louis F. Hartman wrote of the plural form *elohim:* "The odd fact that Hebrew uses a plural noun to designate the sole God of Israel has been explained in various ways. It is not to be understood as a remnant of the polytheism of Abraham's ancestors, or hardly as a 'plural of majesty'—if there is such a thing in Hebrew. Some scholars take it as a plural that expresses an abstract idea (e.g., *zekunim,* 'old age'; *ne'urim,* 'time of youth'), so that *elohim* would really mean 'the Divinity.' More likely, however, it came from Canaanite usage; the early Israelites would have taken over *elohim* as a singular noun, just as they made their own the rest of the Canaanite language."

2   הַיּוֹם — TODAY: The Midrash (collections of rabbinic exegesis) linked this word to Shabbat, with special emphasis to yield: "Today—the Sabbath day—[the world will be saved] if only you would hear His voice." The rabbis said: "If Israel observed one single Shabbat according to its true spirit, deliverance would forthwith ensue" (Babylonian Talmud, *Shabbat* 118b).

3   כִּמְרִיבָה . . . מַסָּה — MERIVAH . . . MASSAH: In Hebrew, *merivah* means "quarrel," and *massah* means "challenge." In the Bible story of the Exodus, Moses gave these two names to a place, Refidim, where the Israelites "challenged and quarreled" with him because of the shortage of water in the wilderness (Exodus 17:1-7). In despair, Moses had appealed to God for support against the revolt. God told him: "I will stand before thee upon the rock in Ḥorev; and thou shalt smite the rock, and there shall come water out of it, that the people may drink." But if this particular trouble was eased by a miracle, "Massah and Merivah" became a catch phrase for being quarrelsome and lacking in faith, which is how the psalmist uses it here.

אֲשֶׁר נִסּוּנִי אֲבוֹתֵיכֶם,	1
בְּחָנוּנִי גַּם רָאוּ פָעֳלִי.	
אַרְבָּעִים שָׁנָה אָקוּט בְּדוֹר	
וָאֹמַר עַם תֹּעֵי לֵבָב הֵם,	
וְהֵם לֹא יָדְעוּ דְרָכָי.	
אֲשֶׁר נִשְׁבַּעְתִּי בְאַפִּי,	2
אִם יְבֹאוּן אֶל מְנוּחָתִי.	

1 When your fathers tried Me, tested Me, even though they saw My work.
For forty years I was wearied with that generation,
and said: It is a people that err in their heart, and they have not known My ways.
2 Where I swore in My wrath that they should not enter into My rest.

נִסּוּנִי — TRIED ME: The idea of God being hurt—or angry—that the Israelites were quick to lose faith in Him when things seemed to be going wrong is one of the anthropomorphisms that abound in the Bible, demanding our understanding. The concept of God is never diminished by the suggestion that He responds to human action in terms that can be personalized. It is, on the contrary, through this approach that the Bible introduced to the Israelites—and through them to the world—the loving relationship between man and God that forms the base for a moral approach to life. Standards of conduct, linked to God's will, were set forth for man to live by. Where he failed, he was made to feel that he had committed a "sin" against the ideal order of life, and that in doing this he had betrayed—and angered—a Being who was as close to him as a parent. In the opposite situation, the spiritual peace that man could achieve through just conduct was an expression of God's "pleasure." 1

נִשְׁבַּעְתִּי בְאַפִּי — I SWORE IN MY WRATH: It has never been easy to trace in human life generally a direct link between moral conduct and God's favor. Jeremiah, among many other Bible writers, expressed this thought (Jeremiah 12:1): "Why does the way of the wicked prosper? Why do all who are treacherous thrive?" The book of Job is one long parable on the difficulty for mankind to understand the problem of "undeserved" human suffering. The answers suggested in the Bible point to the fact that individual events in one person's life offer an inadequate basis for judging the lasting values in human existence. There are no clear answers, yet man has found reassurance in the belief that the world is not a "tale . . . full of sound and fury, signifying nothing." The psalmist tells us (Psalm 92:7) that though evil-doers seem to prosper, "they are doomed to destruction." Isaiah puts less weight on this rationale, and describes the relief that faith brings (Isaiah 40:31): "They who trust the Lord shall renew their strength; they will grow wings like eagles; they shall run and not be weary; they shall march and not be faint." 2

Psalm 96

שִׁירוּ לַייָ שִׁיר חָדָשׁ, 1
שִׁירוּ לַייָ כָּל הָאָרֶץ.
שִׁירוּ לַייָ בָּרְכוּ שְׁמוֹ, 2
בַּשְּׂרוּ מִיּוֹם לְיוֹם יְשׁוּעָתוֹ. 3
סַפְּרוּ בַגּוֹיִם כְּבוֹדוֹ, 4
בְּכָל־הָעַמִּים נִפְלְאוֹתָיו.
כִּי גָדוֹל יְיָ וּמְהֻלָּל מְאֹד,
נוֹרָא הוּא עַל כָּל־אֱלֹהִים.
כִּי כָּל־אֱלֹהֵי הָעַמִּים אֱלִילִים,
וַייָ שָׁמַיִם עָשָׂה.
הוֹד וְהָדָר לְפָנָיו,
עֹז וְתִפְאֶרֶת בְּמִקְדָּשׁוֹ.

1 Sing to the Lord a new song; let all the earth sing to the Lord.
2 Sing to the Lord, bless His Name; proclaim His deliverance day after day.
3 Declare His glory among the nations, His wonders among all peoples.
4 For the Lord is great, endless to praise; awesome in His divinity. The idols of nations are things of nought; the Lord made the heavens. Splendor and beauty attend Him; in His sanctuary, strength and glory.

---

1 שִׁיר חָדָשׁ — A NEW SONG: Was this psalm written to celebrate a new situation—a great deliverance, or perhaps a new reign? There is a parallel in Isaiah 42:10 where the prophet uses the same phrase—"Sing unto the Lord a new song"—to celebrate the redemption from exile in Babylon.

2 בָּרְכוּ שְׁמוֹ — BLESS HIS NAME: According to a biblical tradition, this psalm was sung by King David when the ark of the covenant was brought to Jerusalem after he had founded the city. As described in 1 Chronicles 16, there was a great musical ceremony, including the playing of lutes and harps, the sounding of cymbals, and the blowing of trumpets, after which David recited the poem we know now as this psalm (Psalm 96), together with Psalm 105, and verses from Psalm 106.

3 בַּשְּׂרוּ . . . יְשׁוּעָתוֹ — PROCLAIM HIS DELIVERANCE: That is, "proclaim the deliverance He has secured for us." The word for "proclaim"—*basseru*—has a specially joyous sound—"tell the good tidings." There is certainly a feeling within all these phrases of some great event that has lifted up the hearts of the celebrants.

4 כְּבוֹדוֹ . . . נִפְלְאוֹתָיו — HIS GLORY . . . HIS WONDERS: As so often in the psalms, the glory and wonder of Nature bring home supremely the central truth of the Hebrew faith in One Being who created and sustained the universe. The contrast with paganism was never more clearly expressed than in these few simple verses. Pagan worship included practices that the Hebrews found morally debasing—prostitution, homosexuality, and even child sacrifice; but here the revulsion is *logical*: the pagan gods are merely pieces of wood and stone—idols; the Being we worship "made the Heavens."

הָבוּ לַיְיָ מִשְׁפְּחוֹת עַמִּים, 1
הָבוּ לַיְיָ כָּבוֹד וָעֹז.
הָבוּ לַיְיָ כְּבוֹד שְׁמוֹ,
שְׂאוּ מִנְחָה וּבֹאוּ לְחַצְרוֹתָיו. 2
הִשְׁתַּחֲווּ לַיְיָ בְּהַדְרַת קֹדֶשׁ,
חִילוּ מִפָּנָיו כָּל־הָאָרֶץ.
אִמְרוּ בַגּוֹיִם יְיָ מָלָךְ, 3
אַף תִּכּוֹן תֵּבֵל בַּל תִּמּוֹט,
יָדִין עַמִּים בְּמֵישָׁרִים.
יִשְׂמְחוּ הַשָּׁמַיִם וְתָגֵל הָאָרֶץ,
יִרְעַם הַיָּם וּמְלֹאוֹ.
יַעֲלֹז שָׂדַי וְכָל־אֲשֶׁר בּוֹ,
אָז יְרַנְּנוּ כָּל־עֲצֵי־יָעַר.
לִפְנֵי יְיָ כִּי בָא
כִּי בָא לִשְׁפֹּט הָאָרֶץ,
יִשְׁפֹּט תֵּבֵל בְּצֶדֶק 4
וְעַמִּים בֶּאֱמוּנָתוֹ.

Acclaim to the Lord all races and peoples, acclaim to the Lord honor and strength.
Acclaim to the Lord the glory of His name; bring tribute and enter His courts.
Worship the Lord in the beauty of holiness; let all the earth tremble in His presence.
Declare among the nations: "The Lord rules!" The world is set firm that it cannot be moved. He judges the peoples with equity.
Let the heavens rejoice and the earth be glad! Let the sea roar in its fullness.
Let the fields be glad, and all that is within them; let all the trees of the forest sing for joy before the Lord.
For He comes to judge the earth: He will judge the world in righteousness, and the peoples with equity.

מִשְׁפְּחוֹת עַמִּים — ALL RACES AND PEOPLES: This is one of the innumerable passages in the Bible which assert the universality of the Hebrew conception of God as the central power directing all history. **1**

וּבֹאוּ לְחַצְרוֹתָיו — AND ENTER HIS COURTS: Though the psalm continues to invoke the glory of God for all mankind, this phrase alludes to the worship of God that comes specifically from Israel—worship in the courts of the Temple at Jerusalem. **2**

יְיָ מָלָךְ — THE LORD RULES: God as king in nature is an idea that comes naturally to the psalmist. God is proclaimed not in pagan style as the victor in an annual fertility struggle, but as ruling timelessly over everything in the universe. **3**

יִשְׁפֹּט . . . וְעַמִּים בֶּאֱמוּנָתוֹ — HE WILL JUDGE . . . THE PEOPLES WITH EQUITY: The Bible scholar H. L. Ginsberg has suggested, in an essay on Hebraic hymnody, that the familiar word *yishpot* ("He will judge") means, in this case, "He will provide." "He will provide for the people with graciousness," rather than by a strict judgment. **4**

Psalm 97

יְיָ מָלָךְ תָּגֵל הָאָרֶץ,	1	The Lord reigns; let the earth rejoice; let the multitude of isles be glad.
יִשְׂמְחוּ אִיִּים רַבִּים.		
עָנָן וַעֲרָפֶל סְבִיבָיו,	2	Cloud and mist enfold Him; right and justice are the foundation of His throne.
צֶדֶק וּמִשְׁפָּט מְכוֹן כִּסְאוֹ.		
אֵשׁ לְפָנָיו תֵּלֵךְ,		Fire moves before Him, blazing around His foes.
וּתְלַהֵט סָבִיב צָרָיו.		
הֵאִירוּ בְרָקָיו תֵּבֵל,		His lightning illuminates the world; the earth sees and trembles.
רָאֲתָה וַתָּחֵל הָאָרֶץ.		
הָרִים כַּדּוֹנַג נָמַסּוּ מִלִּפְנֵי יְיָ,		The mountains melt like wax before the Lord, before the Master of all the earth.
מִלִּפְנֵי אֲדוֹן כָּל־הָאָרֶץ.		
הִגִּידוּ הַשָּׁמַיִם צִדְקוֹ,	3	The heavens declare His righteousness; all the peoples behold His glory.
וְרָאוּ כָל־הָעַמִּים כְּבוֹדוֹ.		
יֵבשׁוּ כָּל־עֹבְדֵי פֶסֶל		Ashamed are they who worship graven images, who puff up their pride with hollow gods. False gods, bow down to Him!
הַמִּתְהַלְלִים בָּאֱלִילִים,		
הִשְׁתַּחֲווּ לוֹ כָּל־אֱלֹהִים.		

1 תָּגֵל הָאָרֶץ — LET THE EARTH REJOICE: This is one of the happiest of all the psalms. In these two brief Hebrew words it challenges the concept that Judaism is overwhelmingly concerned with the *fear* of God, with sin and with suffering punishment for it. Certainly our Judaism is stern in one underlying principle: obedience to the moral law. It is unrelenting in the standards of conduct which it demands. It demands rituals and practices which fill a Jew's life. But the goal of faith is not a life bowed down under laws and fears. The beliefs and rituals of Judaism are a means to fulfillment and happiness. A Jew reading this psalm—and so many others like it—is uplifted by the wonder and joy of life and nature, expressing joy in God.

2 עָנָן וַעֲרָפֶל סְבִיבָיו — CLOUD AND MIST ENFOLD HIM: Dispelling the image of a God of wrath, the psalmist evokes a Presence poetic and mystical. In Hebrew, the words for "cloud and mist" (*anan va'arafel*) are themselves gentle and tranquil.

3 הִגִּידוּ הַשָּׁמַיִם צִדְקוֹ — THE HEAVENS DECLARE HIS RIGHTEOUSNESS: One of the joys of reading the Bible is hearing, with a heartwarming sense of familiarity, the frequent echoes of well-known passages. The words here, for example, bring to mind immediately the opening of Psalm 19: "The heavens declare the glory of God, the sky tells of His handiwork."

שָׁמְעָה וַתִּשְׂמַח צִיּוֹן	1	Zion hears and rejoices; the daughters of Judah are glad, because of Your judgments, O Lord.
וַתָּגֵלְנָה בְּנוֹת יְהוּדָה,	2	
לְמַעַן מִשְׁפָּטֶיךָ יְיָ.		For You are supreme over all the earth, exalted above all gods who are worshiped.
כִּי אַתָּה יְיָ עֶלְיוֹן עַל כָּל־הָאָרֶץ,		They who love the Lord hate evil. He guards the souls of His loving ones, delivering them from the hand of the wicked.
מְאֹד נַעֲלֵיתָ עַל כָּל־אֱלֹהִים.		Light dawns for the righteous, joy for the upright in heart.
אֹהֲבֵי יְיָ שִׂנְאוּ רָע		Rejoice in the Lord, you righteous ones, and praise His holy name.
שֹׁמֵר נַפְשׁוֹת חֲסִידָיו,		
מִיַּד רְשָׁעִים יַצִּילֵם.		
אוֹר זָרֻעַ לַצַּדִּיק,		
וּלְיִשְׁרֵי לֵב שִׂמְחָה.		
שִׂמְחוּ צַדִּיקִים בַּיְיָ,	3	
וְהוֹדוּ לְזֵכֶר קָדְשׁוֹ.	4	

שָׁמְעָה וַתִּשְׂמַח צִיּוֹן — ZION HEARS AND REJOICES: These images of happiness come through with additional liveliness in the original because of the flexibility of tenses in biblical Hebrew. Grammatically, the words are in the past tense, as if describing something now over: but in the context of ancient poetic Hebrew the tense of both words conveys an open, endless present, reflecting the timelessness of the feelings expressed in the Bible. **1**

בְּנוֹת יְהוּדָה — THE DAUGHTERS OF JUDAH: In psalmic style, the joy of Zion is paralleled by the happiness of Judah. To give the parallel exact meaning, "daughters" here must suggest territorial dependencies of Judah. This may have been how the poetry was understood when first recited, but it is still pleasant to retain the image of the maidens of Judah singing happily at the wonders vouchsafed to their people. **2**

שִׂמְחוּ צַדִּיקִים בַּיְיָ — REJOICE IN THE LORD, YOU RIGHTEOUS ONES: This last verse of Psalm 97 brings together two key words—*simhu* ("rejoice") and *tzaddikim* ("righteous ones")—in a joyous climax. Throughout the psalm we have heard of God's *tzedakah* ("righteousness"). The *tzaddik*, the just man, strives to emulate God's righteousness. But the life of the *tzaddik* is not to be dour and puritanical. It is to be full of *simhah*—"rejoicing." **3**

וְהוֹדוּ לְזֵכֶר קָדְשׁוֹ — AND PRAISE HIS HOLY NAME: If rendered literally, as in the King James translation version of the Bible, this Hebrew phrase would mean "praise (or give thanks) at the memory of His holiness." This is a satisfying image; but the scholars have suggested, drawing on other parallels, that the Hebrew *lezecher kodsho* has the sense of *leshem kodsho*, as translated here. **4**

מִזְמוֹר 1

שִׁירוּ לַיָי שִׁיר חָדָשׁ 2
כִּי נִפְלָאוֹת עָשָׂה,
הוֹשִׁיעָה לּוֹ יְמִינוֹ
וּזְרוֹעַ קָדְשׁוֹ.
הוֹדִיעַ יְיָ יְשׁוּעָתוֹ, 3
לְעֵינֵי הַגּוֹיִם גִּלָּה צִדְקָתוֹ. 4

1 A Psalm.
2 Sing to the Lord a new song, for
He has done wondrous things,
His right hand and His holy
arm have wrought salvation.
The Lord has made known His
3 power to save; He has revealed
His righteousness to the eyes of
4 the nations.

---

1 מִזְמוֹר — A PSALM: The Hebrew title means "a song." (The English word "psalm" comes from a Greek word *psalmos* which has the same meaning: "a song sung to a harp.") Frequently, the full title of a psalm is *mizmor ledavid*—"a song of David."

2 שִׁיר חָדָשׁ — A NEW SONG: The cry for a new song may indicate, as with Psalm 96, that this was a psalm written to celebrate a special occasion—perhaps "the salvation" spoken of in the opening verses.

3 יְשׁוּעָתוֹ — SALVATION: *Yeshu'ah* ("salvation") is a potent word from a root which means "to deliver." It surfaces repeatedly in the Bible when God saves man, or the people of Israel, by the exercise of His providence. Salvation is God's way of involving Himself with those who seek Him and lean upon His strength, upon "His right hand, and His holy arm." Even if there is no automatic reward for the good life, the psalms show us a God who hears the cry of the poor and desires the well-being of the righteous. The biblical concept seems to be that although man is free to choose between good and evil, God's providence steers him toward goodness.

4 צִדְקָתוֹ — HIS RIGHTEOUSNESS: The Hebrew word, which comes from *tzedakah*, evokes a concept of God which is only partially covered by the English word "righteous." In its full sense, *tzedakah* means action which is right in the sense of "exact" or "fair," a meaning summed up in the English word "just." *Tzedakah* is a criterion of good conduct, especially of kings or other rulers; this attribute of God is repeated over and over in the Bible as the quality which must define the good society. A *tzaddik* is a man whose every action expresses this sense of perfection— "a saint," in human terms. But there is a wider meaning in *tzedakah* as applied to God. One might say that God is seen as putting the world to rights. Out of the primordial chaos, He created a world whose purpose was to radiate His own "rightness." The community of Israel—described in this psalm as *beit yisrael* ("the house of Israel")—has a distinctive role to play in achieving the wholeness—the "rightness"—of this vision. That is why His salvation of Israel as celebrated in this psalm is a revelation of His "rightness"—His righteousness—"to the eyes of all the nations."

זָכַר חַסְדּוֹ וֶאֱמוּנָתוֹ לְבֵית יִשְׂרָאֵל,	1
רָאוּ כָל־אַפְסֵי־אָרֶץ אֵת יְשׁוּעַת אֱלֹהֵינוּ.	2
הָרִיעוּ לַיָי כָּל־הָאָרֶץ, פִּצְחוּ וְרַנְּנוּ וְזַמֵּרוּ.	3
זַמְּרוּ לַיָי בְּכִנּוֹר, בְּכִנּוֹר וְקוֹל זִמְרָה. בַּחֲצֹצְרוֹת וְקוֹל שׁוֹפָר, הָרִיעוּ לִפְנֵי הַמֶּלֶךְ יְיָ. יִרְעַם הַיָם וּמְלֹאוֹ, תֵּבֵל וְיֹשְׁבֵי בָהּ.	
נְהָרוֹת יִמְחֲאוּ כָף, יַחַד הָרִים יְרַנֵּנוּ. לִפְנֵי יְיָ כִּי בָא לִשְׁפֹּט הָאָרֶץ, יִשְׁפֹּט תֵּבֵל בְּצֶדֶק, וְעַמִּים בְּמֵישָׁרִים.	4

He has remembered His loving-kindness and faith to the house of Israel.

The power of our God to save has been manifest to the ends of the earth.

Shout to the Lord in joy, all the earth; break out in songs and psalms.

Sing praises to the Lord with the harp, with the harp and the sound of music.

With trumpets and the sound of the shofar, shout for joy before the Lord, the King.

Let the sea roar in its fullness, the world and all who dwell in it.

Let the rivers clap hands, let the mountains sing together before the Lord.

For He comes to judge the earth; He will judge the world in righteousness, and the peoples with equity.

לְבֵית יִשְׂרָאֵל — TO THE HOUSE OF ISRAEL: The emphasis is on Israel as a community, almost a family, rather than as a state. **1**

כָל־אַפְסֵי־אָרֶץ — THE ENDS OF THE EARTH: This is one more example of how the Bible accommodates and intertwines these two distinct yet related ideas: God's care for mankind and His care for Israel. **2**

פִּצְחוּ וְרַנְּנוּ — BREAK OUT IN SONGS: The musical terms are exhilarating in Hebrew, and all onomatopoeic. *Pitshu* ("break out") has a shattering sound; *hatsotserot* ("trumpets") has the fierceness of trumpets. And similarly exciting is *kol shofar*, the sound of the ram's horn, which raised an alarm, but which also heralded celebration of a momentous event, such as the enthronement of a king. It is in this sense that we hear the *shofar* sounded at Rosh Hashanah, celebrating God as King. **3**

נְהָרוֹת יִמְחֲאוּ כָף — LET THE RIVERS CLAP HANDS: This daring image reminds us irresistibly of other poetic flights of fancy. In Psalm 114, recited at the Seder: "The mountains skipped like rams, the hills like lambs." In Psalm 29 (p. 15): "He makes Lebanon skip like a calf." Here, in Psalm 98, the hills do not skip but sing for joy. **4**

יְיָ מָלָךְ יִרְגְּזוּ עַמִּים,	1
יֹשֵׁב כְּרוּבִים תָּנוּט הָאָרֶץ.	2,3
יְיָ בְּצִיּוֹן גָּדוֹל,	
וְרָם הוּא עַל כָּל־הָעַמִּים.	
יוֹדוּ שִׁמְךָ גָּדוֹל וְנוֹרָא,	
קָדוֹשׁ הוּא.	
וְעֹז מֶלֶךְ מִשְׁפָּט אָהֵב	
אַתָּה כּוֹנַנְתָּ מֵישָׁרִים,	
מִשְׁפָּט וּצְדָקָה בְּיַעֲקֹב	
אַתָּה עָשִׂיתָ.	
רוֹמְמוּ יְיָ אֱלֹהֵינוּ	
וְהִשְׁתַּחֲווּ לַהֲדֹם רַגְלָיו	
קָדוֹשׁ הוּא.	

The Lord reigns; let the peoples tremble.
He is enthroned among the cherubim; the earth shakes.
The Lord is exalted in Zion, high above all the peoples.
They extol His great and awesome name: "He is holy!"
A King in strength, loving justice: It is You who established justice and equity;
You have dealt righteously with Jacob.
Exalt the Lord our God. Bow down to His footstool: "He is holy!"

1   יְיָ מָלָךְ — THE LORD REIGNS: This bold acclaim to God as King is the same as in Psalm 97 (p. 9); yet the identical words can lead to very different forms of expression and worship. In Psalm 97, the words which follow this opening declaration express the happiness of the worshiper: "God is King: let the earth rejoice!" Here, the tone is one of awe: "The Lord reigns: let the peoples tremble."

2   יֹשֵׁב כְּרוּבִים — ENTHRONED AMONG THE CHERUBIM: The ethereal image of "cherubim" was captured in the Temple setting. The cherubim—members of God's heavenly entourage—were part of the decor of the Temple built by King Solomon. According to the detailed description in the Bible (1 Kings 6:23-28) the cherubim were two flying figures with huge outstretched wings: "five cubits was the one wing of the cherub, and five cubits the other wing of the cherub. . . . The wing of one cherub touched one wall, the wing of the other cherub touched the other wall, and their wings touched one another in the midst of the Temple."

3   תָּנוּט הָאָרֶץ — THE EARTH SHAKES: The awesome sight of these huge cherubim symbolized, perhaps, the sudden changes in the elements all too common in the Near East—fierce winds with dark storm clouds. The cherubim were thus a symbolic representation of the power God manifests in nature. The psalmist turns this physical image into a spiritual concept. His words express our sense of human frailty when we contemplate the limitless power of God. The marvel is that this Being, indefinable in essence—"enthroned among the cherubim"—allows His radiance to reach us, at our human level, in love.

מֹשֶׁה וְאַהֲרֹן בְּכֹהֲנָיו	1
וּשְׁמוּאֵל בְּקֹרְאֵי שְׁמוֹ	2
קֹרִאים אֶל יְיָ וְהוּא יַעֲנֵם.	
בְּעַמּוּד עָנָן יְדַבֵּר אֲלֵיהֶם,	
שָׁמְרוּ עֵדֹתָיו וְחֹק נָתַן לָמוֹ.	
יְיָ אֱלֹהֵינוּ אַתָּה עֲנִיתָם,	
אֵל נֹשֵׂא הָיִיתָ לָהֶם,	3
וְנֹקֵם עַל עֲלִילוֹתָם.	
רוֹמְמוּ יְיָ אֱלֹהֵינוּ	
וְהִשְׁתַּחֲווּ לְהַר קָדְשׁוֹ,	4
כִּי קָדוֹשׁ יְיָ אֱלֹהֵינוּ.	

1 Moses and Aaron among His priests, and Samuel who called His name—they called unto the Lord and He answered them.
In a pillar of cloud He spoke to them; they kept His teaching and the Law He gave them.
3 O Lord our God, You answered them; You were a forgiving God to them, avenging their injuries.
4 Exalt the Lord our God, and worship at His holy mountain, for the Lord our God is holy.

בְּכֹהֲנָיו — AMONG HIS PRIESTS: The Hebrew word *kohen* ("priest") has yielded the most common Jewish surname in Jewish life, proudly borne by its inheritors as a sign that they belong to what was once a highly privileged—and responsible—caste. **1**

בְּקֹרְאֵי שְׁמוֹ — WHO CALLED HIS NAME: In the tradition ascribed to Moses in the books of Leviticus and Numbers, the Hebrew priesthood had developed a core of great spirituality. This was due especially to the High Priest, whose duties generated a sense of unique closeness to God. On the Day of Atonement, he alone went into the Holy of Holies, the innermost and most sacred room of the Temple, to carry out the rituals of purification for the whole people. **2**

אֵל נֹשֵׂא — A FORGIVING GOD: The same thought is defined at length in one of the most dramatic of all the psalms—Psalm 18—where the poet, bowed down in personal anguish, finds God's blessing coming to him out of the most terrifying manifestation of God's power—a storm of stupendous proportions. "In my distress," the psalmist says, "I called upon the Lord." God's first response was in the form of a storm: "Then the earth shook and trembled: the foundations of the mountains moved and were shaken. . . . He bowed down the heavens also, and darkness was under His feet. . . . Mounted on a cherub, He flew, gliding on the wings of the wind." Yet, out of the storm God answered in terms of love (Psalm 18:17-20): "He sent from above, He took me, He drew me out of many waters . . . because He delighted in me." **3**

לְהַר קָדְשׁוֹ — HIS HOLY MOUNTAIN: Everything involved with God is graced with His holiness. This ideal is even expected of the entire people Israel. The "Holiness Code" (Leviticus 17-26) repeats a dozen times in different formulations the striking call to the nation: "You shall be holy, for I the Lord your God am holy." **4**

Psalm 29		
מִזְמוֹר לְדָוִד הָבוּ לַיָי בְּנֵי אֵלִים, הָבוּ לַיָי כָּבוֹד וָעֹז. הָבוּ לַיָי כְּבוֹד שְׁמוֹ, הִשְׁתַּחֲווּ לַיָי בְּהַדְדַת קֹדֶשׁ.		A Psalm of David. Acclaim for the Lord, O beings on high, acclaim for the Lord His glory and strength. Acclaim for the Lord the glory of His name; worship the Lord in the beauty of holiness.
קוֹל יְיָ עַל הַמָּיִם,	1	The voice of the Lord is over the waters; the God of glory
אֵל הַכָּבוֹד הִרְעִים	2	thunders—the Lord is over the
יְיָ עַל־מַיִם רַבִּים.	3	mighty waters.

1   קוֹל יְיָ — THE VOICE OF THE LORD: The style of this psalm is distinctive: short phrases, repeated with urgency and excitement. The key phrase is "the voice of the Lord"—it is repeated seven times. Some say that this is why this psalm is included in this service—the repeated phrase corresponds to the seven days of the week, which culminates in Shabbat.

2   אֵל הַכָּבוֹד הִרְעִים — THE GLORY OF GOD THUNDERS: The whole earth is convulsed in storm, and then, suddenly, it is over, and a sweet serenity fills the air. The whole episode symbolizes God's relationship to man. His power in nature fills us with awe and exultation, but we look to Him for the serenity which follows.

3   מַיִם רַבִּים — THE MIGHTY WATERS: The phrase conjures up the ever-absorbing mystery of creation, when "darkness was upon the face of the deep, and the spirit of God hovered over the face of the waters" (Genesis 1:2). In a different way, it takes us back, through its imagery, to the myths of the ancient Near Eastern world, more than 3,000 years ago, when the Hebrews were becoming a people, and defining their religious faith in contrast to the paganism of the world around them. A major pagan myth dealt with the sea god (the god of "mighty waters") who was defeated annually by the god of fertility, to allow nature to revive. The genius of Hebrew religion was that although it retained some of the pagan *imagery*, it replaced the pagan *myth* with the concept of a single, all-powerful God through whom nature is fulfilled perpetually, without the absurdity of annual battles among minor gods.

PARALLELS AND CONTRASTS: The contrast was seen at Ras Shamra in Syria in 1928 when excavation revealed the abundant archives of the merchant city Ugarit. Ugarit had flourished from the middle of the fourteenth century B.C.E. until its collapse before the Hittites early in the twelfth century B.C.E., roughly the time of the Exodus. The scholar H. L. Ginsberg, of The Jewish Theological Seminary of America, was the first to recognize the linguistic parallels between Psalm 29 and one of the Ras Shamra hymns, even though the psalmist has completely transformed the religious intent of the imagery.

קוֹל יְיָ בַּכֹּחַ, קוֹל יְיָ בֶּהָדָר. קוֹל יְיָ שֹׁבֵר אֲרָזִים, וַיְשַׁבֵּר יְיָ אֶת־אַרְזֵי הַלְּבָנוֹן. וַיַּרְקִידֵם כְּמוֹ עֵגֶל, לְבָנוֹן וְשִׂרְיוֹן כְּמוֹ בֶן רְאֵמִים. קוֹל יְיָ חֹצֵב לַהֲבוֹת אֵשׁ. קוֹל יְיָ יָחִיל מִדְבָּר, יָחִיל יְיָ מִדְבַּר קָדֵשׁ. קוֹל יְיָ יְחוֹלֵל אַיָּלוֹת, וַיֶּחֱשֹׂף יְעָרוֹת וּבְהֵיכָלוֹ כֻּלּוֹ אֹמֵר כָּבוֹד. יְיָ לַמַּבּוּל יָשָׁב, וַיֵּשֶׁב יְיָ מֶלֶךְ לְעוֹלָם. יְיָ עֹז לְעַמּוֹ יִתֵּן, יְיָ יְבָרֵךְ אֶת־עַמּוֹ בַשָּׁלוֹם.	The voice of the Lord in power; the voice of the Lord in majesty. The voice of the Lord breaks the cedars; the Lord has shattered the cedars of Lebanon. He makes Lebanon skip like a calf, Sirion like a young ox. The voice of the Lord kindles flames of fire. The voice of the Lord whirls the desert; the Lord whirls the desert of Kadesh. The voice of the Lord makes the hinds writhe and strips the forests bare, while His Temple speaks of glory. The Lord sat enthroned at the flood, and sits as king forever. The Lord will give strength to His people; the Lord will bless His people with peace.

בֶּהָדָר — IN MAJESTY: This Hebrew word for majesty is archaic and carries with it an indefinable aura of splendor.

לְבָנוֹן וְשִׂרְיוֹן — LEBANON . . . SIRION: These place-names are used in exactly the same way as in the Ugaritic hymn analyzed by Ginsberg (see p. 15). From this ancient parallel it can be shown that "the desert of Kadesh" refers to Kadesh on the Orontes river nearby.

לַמַּבּוּל יָשָׁב — ENTHRONED AT THE FLOOD: This evokes a fully Hebraic concept of God at creation, or at the time of the great flood; yet in the parallel Ugaritic hymn, it refers to the Canaanite god Baal, who defeated the sea-god *Yam* ("Sea") in the annual fertility battle.

עֹז לְעַמּוֹ — STRENGTH TO HIS PEOPLE: After the cosmic power of the imagery so far, this final verse establishes the direct relationship of the Creator to "His people," Israel. It is this link between God and Israel which is the the ultimate meaning of this psalm. The rabbis saw this psalm as a description of the world at the time of the revelation at Mt. Sinai. They saw a progression of three themes running through all these Shabbat evening psalms: (1) the exultation of God's power in nature, (2) the love of God for mankind, and (3) the realization of God's love, exemplified in the awesome and dramatic giving of the Torah ("strength") to Israel.

Shabbat is hailed in this beloved sixteenth-century
song, which draws allusions from the Bible
and from legend to celebrate the happiness of the day.
In Hebrew, the style is light-hearted, full
of engaging rhymes and puns.

LECHAH DODI

לְכָה דוֹדִי

לְכָה דוֹדִי לִקְרַאת כַּלָּה
פְּנֵי שַׁבָּת נְקַבְּלָה.

Come, my beloved, to meet the
bride:
come to greet the Sabbath.

שָׁמוֹר וְזָכוֹר בְּדִבּוּר אֶחָד 1
הִשְׁמִיעָנוּ אֵל הַמְיֻחָד, 2
יְיָ אֶחָד וּשְׁמוֹ אֶחָד
לְשֵׁם וּלְתִפְאֶרֶת וְלִתְהִלָּה. 3

"Keep" and "Remember"—a single
command, which God—in
unity—caused us to hear.
The Lord is One and His name is
One, to His renown, His glory
and His praise.

Lechah dodi likrat kallah, penei shabbat nekabbelah.

LECHAH DODI: The idea of Shabbat as a bride, radiating joy, goes back to talmudic times. Among the mystics who thronged Safed in sixteenth-century Palestine, ideas of this kind were celebrated with passionate intensity. An English scholar, Israel Abrahams, in a commentary on this song, evokes well the mood on the eve of Shabbat. As dusk approached, he writes, "white-robed men and boys sang in the Sabbath to the strains of the Song of Songs, going in procession up the hills and down the dales, chanting psalms, and calling on the bride to enter her loved one's home."

AUTHORSHIP: The song was composed by the poet Solomon Halevi Alkabets (1505–76), who settled early in life among the mystics of Safed in Galilee. He reveals his name—*Shelomo Halevi*—in the form of an acrostic, with each letter beginning successive verses of the song.

VARIETIES OF HEBREW POETRY: Hebrew poetry, profuse in the Bible in numerous ancient forms, followed more systematic patterns later as the writers came under new influences. In the Bible, the poets and prophets used a majestic— often archaic—vocabulary, and drew on stress and parallelism for effect.

1 שָׁמוֹר וְזָכוֹר — "KEEP" AND "REMEMBER": In each of the two versions of the Ten Commandments in the Bible (Exodus 20 and Deuteronomy 5), a different word begins the fourth commandment, the commandment enjoining observance of Shabbat. But the two are "one utterance" (*dibbur eḥad*), the poet says, echoing a saying of the rabbis (in the *Mechilta*) that the two versions of the Ten Commandments were spoken simultaneously, as "one utterance."

2 אֵל הַמְיֻחָד — GOD IN UNITY: The poet invents this Hebrew phrase to express God's existence in a kind of infrangible unity.

3 לְשֵׁם — TO HIS RENOWN: Hebrew *shem* has a wider meaning than "name." The word is used most distinctively in itself as a respectful way of referring to God: *Hashem*—"The Name."

17

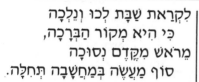

לִקְרַאת שַׁבָּת לְכוּ וְנֵלְכָה
כִּי הִיא מְקוֹר הַבְּרָכָה,
מֵרֹאשׁ מִקֶּדֶם נְסוּכָה
סוֹף מַעֲשֶׂה בְּמַחֲשָׁבָה תְּחִלָּה. 1

מִקְדַּשׁ מֶלֶךְ עִיר מְלוּכָה 2
קוּמִי צְאִי מִתּוֹךְ הַהֲפֵכָה,
רַב-לָךְ שֶׁבֶת בְּעֵמֶק הַבָּכָא 3
וְהוּא יַחֲמֹל עָלַיִךְ חֶמְלָה.

הִתְנַעֲרִי מֵעָפָר קוּמִי 4
לִבְשִׁי בִּגְדֵי תִפְאַרְתֵּךְ עַמִּי,
עַל-יַד בֶּן יִשַׁי בֵּית הַלַּחְמִי
קָרְבָה אֶל נַפְשִׁי גְּאָלָהּ.

Come, let us go to meet the
Sabbath, for it is a fountain of
blessing;
From the beginning, from of old,
it was ordained; last in act,
first in thought.

The royal shrine, regal city, rise and
come forth from destruction.
Too long have you dwelt in the vale
of tears: now God will show His
pity on you.

Awake, arise from the dust; array
yourself, O my people, in
splendor;
At hand is Bethlehem's David,
Jesse's son, bringing deliverance
into my life.

Lechah dodi likrat kallah, penei shabbat nekabbelah.

בְּמַחֲשָׁבָה תְּחִלָּה — FIRST IN THOUGHT: Shabbat came at the end of Creation, 1
but existed in God's plan before the work began. The Torah is often spoken of in
the same way, as having existed before creation as the epitome of wisdom—God's
plan for the universe.

עִיר מְלוּכָה — REGAL CITY: The poem now turns to "the regal city," Jerusalem, 2
and bids it arise from its destruction to become a fitting abode for the Queen-Bride—
Shabbat. These are messianic passages, heralding the rebuilding of the Temple and
the return of the Jews from exile. Throughout the song the poet draws on phrases
from the Bible—fully familiar to his audience—to express the longing for the
restoration of Zion.

עֵמֶק הַבָּכָא — THE VALE OF TEARS: This is a phrase taken from Psalm 84:7, 3
where the word בָּכָא probably means "balsam-tree." The poet makes a pun here,
using the word as if it were related to בָּכָה, "weeping." The whole passage of the
original psalm is obscure, translated variously as "the valley of Baca," or "the
thirsty valley." But "the vale of tears" is an acceptable image as part of this poem.

מֵעָפָר קוּמִי — ARISE FROM THE DUST: These two lines of the stanza are a direct 4
quotation of the first two verses of the fifty-second chapter of Isaiah, in reverse
order. Indeed, for the rest of the poem until the last stanza, verses from Isaiah are
the major source for the rhapsodic expression of hope that the poet seeks to

18

הִתְעוֹרְרִי הִתְעוֹרְרִי
כִּי בָא אוֹרֵךְ קוּמִי אוֹרִי,
עוּרִי עוּרִי שִׁיר דַּבֵּרִי
כְּבוֹד יְיָ עָלַיִךְ נִגְלָה. | 1 | Awake, awake, for your light has
come. Arise, shine!
Awake, awake, give forth in song;
the glory of the Lord is revealed
to you.

לֹא תֵבוֹשִׁי וְלֹא תִכָּלְמִי
מַה־תִּשְׁתּוֹחֲחִי וּמַה־תֶּהֱמִי,
בָּךְ יֶחֱסוּ עֲנִיֵּי עַמִּי
וְנִבְנְתָה עִיר עַל תִּלָּהּ. | 2 | Be not ashamed, be not confused;
no longer humbled, no longer
sighing;
The poor of my people trust in Thee;
and the city shall be builded on
her own mound.

Lechah dodi likrat kallah, penei shabbat nekabbelah.

---

express, to match the high spirits that are generated by the celebration of Shabbat. Of the three major prophets who had confronted the disaster of exile in Babylon, Isaiah was always the one whose vision of the future offered to Jews a completely convincing picture of the reversal of the agony. The prophet Jeremiah was a man of sorrow, even if his personal authority conveyed human dignity and courage. The prophet Ezekiel, looking to the future, was wrapped up in a sense of mystery. In contemplating Israel's fate, Ezekiel drew powerfully on the deep appeal of the ancient priestly system; but beyond that, he expressed the overwhelming power in the idea of God, to which he responded in wild, bewildering visions, capturing an ecstasy attuned to the mystery of creation. It was the prophet Isaiah who spoke always in human terms, bringing balm to the soul. With marvelous assurance, Isaiah saw failures transformed into a message of comfort and hope. At one with God, Isaiah prophesied that God would radiate His message from a restored Jerusalem. It would never be easy for man to fulfill this vision, but one lived in hope. "Break forth into joy," he had cried. "Sing together, ye waste place of Jerusalem." *Lechah Dodi* is a reflection of the same spirit.

1 | כִּי בָא אוֹרֵךְ — FOR YOUR LIGHT HAS COME: This is from Isaiah 60:1, perhaps the most poetic of all his messages of hope: "Arise, shine, for thy light is come, and the glory of the Lord is risen upon thee."

2 | מַה־תִּשְׁתּוֹחֲחִי — NO LONGER HUMBLED: Literally: "Why do you cast yourself down?" The unusual formation of the Hebrew is a direct echo of a moving passage in Psalm 42:6, where the psalmist tries to lift up his spirit through faith: "Why are you cast down, my soul?" (*mah tishtohahi nafshi*); "Have hope in God—I will yet praise Him for His saving presence." The psalmist has felt that for all his faith, peace of mind has eluded him. He has turned desperately to God in wild, far-off places—"in the land of Jordan and Hermon, on Mount Mizar"—but still there

19

וְהָיוּ לִמְשִׁסָּה שֹׁאסָיִךְ
וְרָחֲקוּ כָּל־מְבַלְּעָיִךְ,
יָשִׂישׂ עָלַיִךְ אֱלֹהָיִךְ
כִּמְשׂושׂ חָתָן עַל כַּלָּה. 1

They who spoiled you shall be
    spoiled, your devourers shall go
    far away;
Then God shall rejoice over thee,
    as a bridgroom rejoices over his
    bride.

יָמִין וּשְׂמֹאל תִּפְרוֹצִי
וְאֶת־יְיָ תַּעֲרִיצִי,
עַל־יַד אִישׁ בֶּן פַּרְצִי
וְנִשְׂמְחָה וְנָגִילָה. 2

You will break free, right and left;
    you will reverence the Lord;
Through the offspring of Perez,
    we also shall rejoice and be glad.

בּוֹאִי בְשָׁלוֹם עֲטֶרֶת בַּעְלָהּ
גַּם בְּשִׂמְחָה וּבְצָהֳלָה,
תּוֹךְ אֱמוּנֵי עַם סְגֻלָּה 3
בּוֹאִי כַלָּה בּוֹאִי כַלָּה. 4

Come in peace, crown of her
    husband, in gladness and joy.
Amid the faithful of the treasured
    people, come O bride, come
    O bride.

Lechah dodi likrat kallah, penei shabbat nekabbelah.

---

seems to be no hope. "Deep calls unto deep," he says. "All Your waves and billows have swept over me." In this Shabbat song, however, the exact words of the psalm are transformed by the joy that Shabbat generates into an assurance of happiness. The poet of *Lechah Dodi* is no longer "ashamed and confused," no long "humbled and sighing."

וְרָחֲקוּ כָּל־מְבַלְּעָיִךְ — YOUR DEVOURERS SHALL GO FAR AWAY: No transla- 1
tion can express the powerful rhythm of the words in Hebrew, nor the captivating rhymes: *shosayich, mevalayich, elohayich.* The whole of *Lechah Dodi* is inspired this way. In the next verse, the rhymes are even more ingenious: *tifrotsi, ta'aritsi, ben partsi.*

אִישׁ בֶּן פַּרְצִי — OFFSPRING OF PEREZ: This is another messianic reference, for 2
the Messiah is to be a descendant of King David. In the Bible, Perez was an ancestor of Boaz, husband of Ruth, from whom David was descended (Ruth 4:18).

עַם סְגֻלָּה — TREASURED PEOPLE: This phrase has led to confusion; it was mis- 3
leadingly translated in the old English of the King James version (Deuteronomy 14:2) as "peculiar people." The translators meant "peculiar" as "special to God," which is how they translated the same words in Deuteronomy 7:6. *Segullah* is from a Hebrew root meaning "treasure."

בּוֹאִי כַלָּה — COME O BRIDE: Most of us know the word for "bride" as כַּלָּה 4
(*kallah*). Here, the Hebrew is *bo'i challah,* with a soft כ (*ch*). This is because the first letter כ (*k*) which would have been "hard," is softened after a vowel.

Unlike the psalms which contemplate the
dramas of nature and the cosmic forces of the
universe, this Shabbat psalm is quiet,
confident, and radiantly joyous, in the ideal
spirit of Shabbat itself.

SABBATH PSALM

שִׁיר לְיוֹם שַׁבָּת

Psalm 92		

מִזְמוֹר שִׁיר לְיוֹם הַשַּׁבָּת. **1** — A Psalm for the Sabbath Day.

טוֹב לְהוֹדוֹת לַיָי, **2** — It is good to give thanks to the Lord,
to sing hymns to Your name,
O Most High.

וּלְזַמֵּר לְשִׁמְךָ עֶלְיוֹן. — To declare Your love in the
morning, and Your constancy at night

לְהַגִּיד בַּבֹּקֶר חַסְדֶּךָ,
וֶאֱמוּנָתְךָ בַּלֵּילוֹת.

עֲלֵי עָשׂוֹר וַעֲלֵי נָבֶל, — To the music of lute and lyre,
the plangent sound of the harp.

עֲלֵי הִגָּיוֹן בְּכִנּוֹר.

כִּי שִׂמַּחְתַּנִי יְיָ בְּפָעֳלֶךָ, — For you rejoice me with Your deeds,
O Lord;

בְּמַעֲשֵׂי יָדֶיךָ אֲרַנֵּן. **3** — I sing out for the works of Your
hands.

מַה־גָּדְלוּ מַעֲשֶׂיךָ יְיָ, — How great are Your works, O Lord,
how deep Your thoughts.

מְאֹד עָמְקוּ מַחְשְׁבֹתֶיךָ.

אִישׁ בַּעַר לֹא יֵדָע, **4** — The fool will never learn, the
dullard never understand

וּכְסִיל לֹא יָבִין אֶת־זֹאת. — That though the wicked flourish
like grass, and the evil-doers prosper,

בִּפְרֹחַ רְשָׁעִים כְּמוֹ עֵשֶׂב
וַיָּצִיצוּ כָּל־פֹּעֲלֵי אָוֶן,

לְהִשָּׁמְדָם עֲדֵי עַד. **5** — Yet they are doomed to destruction.

---

1 מִזְמוֹר שִׁיר לְיוֹם הַשַּׁבָּת — A PSALM FOR THE SABBATH DAY: There is a beautiful comment on this poem in the Mishnah (edited in the second century C.E.): "On the Shabbat, the Levites sang this psalm [Psalm 92]—a song for the time that is to come, for the day that shall be totally Shabbat and rest in the life everlasting."

2 טוֹב לְהוֹדוֹת — IT IS GOOD TO GIVE THANKS: The rabbis said in a delightful midrash that Adam sang this psalm in gratitude after his first night on earth, i.e., on the first Shabbat of all.

3 בְּמַעֲשֵׂי יָדֶיךָ — FOR THE WORKS OF YOUR HANDS: A Jew tries to absorb mystically what is ultimately inexpressible in words: that the universe came into being by the will of God. In a moment of prayer, we reach out from the finite to the Infinite.

4 אִישׁ בַּעַר לֹא יֵדָע — THE FOOL WILL NEVER LEARN: In Hebrew, an archaic expression: *ish ba'ar* ("a man of brutishness").

5 לְהִשָּׁמְדָם עֲדֵי עַד — THEY ARE DOOMED TO DESTRUCTION: We met this thought earlier in discussing Psalm 95 (p. 4). Ultimately, evil ends.

21

וְאַתָּה מָרוֹם לְעֹלָם יְיָ.
כִּי הִנֵּה אֹיְבֶיךָ יְיָ
כִּי הִנֵּה אֹיְבֶיךָ יֹאבֵדוּ,
יִתְפָּרְדוּ כָּל־פֹּעֲלֵי אָוֶן.
וַתָּרֶם כִּרְאֵים קַרְנִי,
בַּלֹּתִי בְּשֶׁמֶן רַעֲנָן.
וַתַּבֵּט עֵינִי בְּשׁוּרָי,
בַּקָּמִים עָלַי מְרֵעִים
תִּשְׁמַעְנָה אָזְנָי.
צַדִּיק כַּתָּמָר יִפְרָח,
כְּאֶרֶז בַּלְּבָנוֹן יִשְׂגֶּה.
שְׁתוּלִים בְּבֵית יְיָ,
בְּחַצְרוֹת אֱלֹהֵינוּ יַפְרִיחוּ
עוֹד יְנוּבוּן בְּשֵׂיבָה,
דְּשֵׁנִים וְרַעֲנַנִּים יִהְיוּ.
לְהַגִּיד כִּי יָשָׁר יְיָ,
צוּרִי וְלֹא עַוְלָתָה בּוֹ.

But you are exalted forever, O Lord.
See how Your enemies, O Lord,
see how Your enemies perish,
how the evil-doers are scattered.
You lift my head high like a wild ox,
   anointing me richly with oil.
My eyes saw the defeat of my
   enemies;
when they rose to harm me,
   my ears heard their end.
The righteous shall flourish like the
   palm tree,
grow tall like a cedar of Lebanon.
Planted in the House of the Lord,
   they shall flourish in the courts
   of our God.
Fruitful still in old age, luxuriant
   and ever-green,
Proclaiming that the Lord is just—
   my Rock, in whom there is no
   wrong.

יִתְפָּרְדוּ כָּל־פֹּעֲלֵי אָוֶן — THE EVIL-DOERS ARE SCATTERED: The English scholar Israel Abrahams said on this passage: "The ultimate triumph of right over wrong is an essential element in the divine ordering of things."

וַתָּרֶם כִּרְאֵים קַרְנִי — YOU LIFT MY HEAD HIGH LIKE A WILD OX: This phrase, expressing fierceness and strength, may be an echo of the same phrase in the poetic testament of Moses when he blessed the tribe of Joseph (Deuteronomy 33:17): "His glory shall be like the firstling of his bullock, his horns are like the horns of the wild ox."

בְּשׁוּרָי — THE DEFEAT OF MY ENEMIES: This psalm may have been composed to celebrate a specific military victory in ancient times.

כַּתָּמָר יִפְרָח — FLOURISH LIKE THE PALM TREE: In this powerful image, the worshiper at the Temple—"the courts of our God"—stands free and upright with the soaring strength of the palm tree. It brings to mind immediately the beautiful description, in Psalm 1 (p. 3), of the fulfillment of the godly man: "He shall be like a tree planted by the water, that brings forth fruit in season. His life shall not wither, and whatsoever he does shall prosper."

Psalm 93

יְיָ מָלָךְ גֵּאוּת לָבֵשׁ
לָבֵשׁ יְיָ עֹז הִתְאַזָּר, 1

אַף תִּכּוֹן תֵּבֵל בַּל תִּמּוֹט. 2
נָכוֹן כִּסְאֲךָ מֵאָז, מֵעוֹלָם אָתָּה.
נָשְׂאוּ נְהָרוֹת יְיָ
נָשְׂאוּ נְהָרוֹת קוֹלָם,
יִשְׂאוּ נְהָרוֹת דָּכְיָם.
מִקֹּלוֹת מַיִם רַבִּים
אַדִּירִים מִשְׁבְּרֵי־יָם,
אַדִּיר בַּמָּרוֹם יְיָ.
עֵדֹתֶיךָ נֶאֶמְנוּ מְאֹד,
לְבֵיתְךָ נַאֲוָה־קֹדֶשׁ
יְיָ לְאֹרֶךְ יָמִים.

1 The Lord reigns, clothed in pride;
the Lord has girded Himself in
strength.
2 The world is set firm, it cannot be
moved;
Your throne is set firm from old:
You are Eternity.
The floods lift up, O Lord, they lift
their voices;
the floods lift up their pounding.
Above the thunder of mighty
waters, the majesty of the
breakers of the sea,
the Lord is majestic on high.
Your witness is very sure;
Your House has the beauty of
holiness,
O Lord, as long as time endures.

In some congregations the Mourners' Kaddish (p. 79) is
recited at this time.

---

1 יְיָ מָלָךְ — THE LORD REIGNS: Psalms which emphasize God as "king" have been
interpreted by some scholars to be perhaps echoes of ancient annual fertility
festivals (mentioned above, p. 15), at which the triumphant god was enthroned.
They would point, in this psalm, to the triumph over *Yam* (the sea god), as
expressed in the verse: "above the thunder of mighty waters, the majesty of the
breakers of the sea." But this is just one more example of imagery surviving in
poetry, with the meaning transformed. It is God's permanent force in nature that
is being celebrated in these psalms.

2 תִּכּוֹן תֵּבֵל — THE WORLD IS SET FIRM: Like Psalm 92 (p. 21) and many other
elements of the Shabbat liturgy, this short but powerful hymn proclaims the
majesty of creation. But here the focus changes from the act of creation to the
purpose behind the creation. The universe was created with principle and purpose;
the world "is set firm, it cannot be moved." We have a sense of a fixed order that
flows from the will and the word of God. In rabbinic terminology, the "word"
which heralded creation was not speech as we know it but the *principle* of the
universe, embracing not merely the laws of nature but the moral law that is part of
the same single act of creation: "By the word of God the heavens were made, and
all their hosts by the breath of His mouth. . . . He spoke, and it was; He commanded and the world stood firm" (Psalm 33:6, 9).

23

This call to worship— "bless the Lord"—will
lead us into the moment when we recite the
Sh'ma. We come to it slowly, through opening
our minds to the truths that come to us
"when we lie down to sleep and when we rise."

BARECHU

בָּרְכוּ

The ḥazzan says:		
בָּרְכוּ אֶת־יְיָ הַמְבֹרָךְ.	1,2	Bless the Lord, who is to be blessed.
We respond:		
בָּרוּךְ יְיָ הַמְבֹרָךְ לְעוֹלָם וָעֶד.	3	Blessed is the Lord, who is to be blessed forever and ever.

Baruch adonai hamevorach le'olam va'ed.

BARECHU: We approach the recital of the *Sh'ma* with a ritual established 2,000 years ago. The Mishnah, the second-century rabbinic code, tells us to preface and to follow the *Sh'ma* in the evening service with special blessings, two before it and two after it. As we shall see, each of these ancient blessings affirms thoughts about God that surface with deep power at eventide.

בָּרְכוּ אֶת־יְיָ — BLESS THE LORD: Why do we bless God, praise Him, pray to Him? If God is infinite in power, does He need our worship? Can He be affected by our words? Some teachers have explained that as we worship God, it is we who are transformed. We reach out to the mystery of the universe, and in the words we frame, our own lives are graced with its mystery. [1]

הַמְבֹרָךְ — WHO IS TO BE BLESSED: The idea of putting the emphasis on our human need, as explained in the paragraph above, was discussed by the English philosopher Louis Jacobs in his book *A Jewish Theology*. On the benefit of worship to man, he quotes the great medieval scholar Naḥmanides (1194–c. 1270): "The advantage which results from the observance of the precepts is not to God Himself but to keep mankind from evil beliefs or ugly character traits . . . to remind us of the wonders of the Creator . . . to make the truth known to us and remind us of it all the time." [2]

לְעוֹלָם וָעֶד — FOREVER AND EVER: Louis Jacobs also explores a more mystical approach, one linked to the Kabbalah. The Kabbalah, as he explains, sees the worship of God extending far beyond an ordinary lifespan. The Kabbalists argue that God needs worship as part of His plan for the universe. He has given humanity the cosmic task of causing the divine grace to flow through all creation. "For the Kabbalists, it is not alone the effect on the human character produced by the deed which is significant. The deed itself has a semi-magical aim." When we serve God, "it sets in motion benevolent forces 'on high' and helps to promote cosmic grace and harmony." Very few of us, says Jacobs, believe in the reality of this Kabbalist scheme, "but may it not serve as a reminder that worship evokes a reaching-out for the Infinite?" To think of prayer as "directed solely towards the immediate satisfaction of human needs" is to belittle it. "Perhaps the deepest human need is the worship of the Highest, with human fulfillment dependent on a relationship with the Creator." [3]

This is the first of the two blessings that
lead us to the recital of the *Sh'ma,* in the ritual laid
down in the Mishnah, as explained on p. **24.**

MA'ARIV ARAVIM

מַעֲרִיב עֲרָבִים

בָּרוּךְ אַתָּה יְיָ אֱלֹהֵינוּ מֶלֶךְ הָעוֹלָם, אֲשֶׁר בִּדְבָרוֹ מַעֲרִיב עֲרָבִים. 1,2 בְּחָכְמָה פּוֹתֵחַ שְׁעָרִים, 3 וּבִתְבוּנָה מְשַׁנֶּה עִתִּים, 4 וּמַחֲלִיף אֶת־הַזְּמַנִּים.	We offer a blessing to the Lord, our God, King of the universe, through whose word we come to the evening twilight. In His divine wisdom, He opens the gates of dawn; with His understanding, He changes times and varies the seasons.

1 אֲשֶׁר בִּדְבָרוֹ — THROUGH WHOSE WORD: As we noted earlier (p. 23), the "word" of God is not speech, but the power through which the universe was brought into being. An ancient blessing which opens the morning service expresses this thought dramatically: *baruch she'amar vehayah ha'olom* ("Blessed is He who spoke, and the universe came into being."). The concept of "the word" as the creative power of God appears in Greek as *logos,* and in Aramaic as *memra.* In rabbinic thought it covers the divine wisdom of God through which the universe is ordered, and the divine Presence—the *shechinah.*

2 מַעֲרִיב עֲרָבִים — WE COME TO THE EVENING TWILIGHT: These two words (*ma'ariv aravim*), very soft to the ear in Hebrew, have the literal sense of "who has evened the evening." The rabbis in talmudic times were imbued with the grandeur of the Bible's language, and used it creatively to express their feelings of God's grace. In this instance, the word *erev* ("evening") is turned into a verb (*ma'ariv*), and used to convey the thought of God as a force sustaining and permeating the universe continuously.

3 פּוֹתֵחַ שְׁעָרִים — HE OPENS THE GATES: This beautiful passage takes us through the magical transformation of a single day, starting with the opening of "the gates of heaven" at dawn, and moving on through the changing of "times and seasons" until we see the stars at night, spread out in the firmament "according to his plan." As we murmur these words of praise, God's soothing, unfailing renewal of nature comes home to us, affirmed here in the closing words of the blessing: "who has led us to the evening twilight"—*ma'ariv aravim.*

4 וּבִתְבוּנָה — WITH HIS UNDERSTANDING: The Hebrew word *tevunah* ("understanding") is a parallel with *hochmah* ("wisdom") in the preceding phrase, but perhaps with an added weight, conveying the concept of God's "intelligence," His "understanding" of the subtle interconnections within nature, and between nature and humanity.

וּמְסַדֵּר אֶת־הַכּוֹכָבִים	1	He sets the stars in order in their courses
בְּמִשְׁמְרוֹתֵיהֶם	2	
בָּרָקִיעַ, כִּרְצוֹנוֹ.	3,4	In the firmament, according to His plan.

וּמְסַדֵּר אֶת־הַכּוֹכָבִים — HE SETS THE STARS IN ORDER: The Hebrew word *mesadder* ("sets in order") is from the same root which gives us the word *siddur* for the prayerbook, and *seder* for the order of service at the Eve of Passover meal. **1**

בְּמִשְׁמְרוֹתֵיהֶם — IN THEIR COURSES: The Hebrew word for "course"—*mishmeret* (from the word *shamar*, "to keep" or "to keep watch")—poetically conveys the idea of stars in ordered attendance on God in heaven. As always in the ancient prayers, the images flow from the Bible. In this case, "the stars in order in their courses" brings to mind the vision of the seer Micaiah when summoned to read the omens by King Jehoshaphat (1 Kings 22:19): "I see God sitting on His throne, and all the hosts of heaven standing by Him on His right hand and on His left." There is the same thought in Psalm 103:19-21: "The Lord has prepared His throne in the heavens. . . . Bless the Lord, ye His angels . . . bless the Lord, all ye His hosts . . . that do His pleasure." The Bible scholar Theodore H. Gaster explains that "host" (*tzeva*) is used here in the technical sense of "palace corps." The same term is used in earlier Mesopotamian archives, "reflecting the widespread ancient notion that things on earth have their counterpart in heaven." The stars, as celestial beings, "are portrayed as a formal militia, marshaled and commanded by God." Isaiah echoed this tone in a poetic passage (Isaiah 40:26): "Lift up your eyes and see: who created these? Who is it that leads forth His host by roster, summoning each by name?" **2**

בָּרָקִיעַ — IN THE FIRMAMENT: The Hebrew word *rakia* means, literally, "an extended surface"—the vault of heaven. But the King James version translation of *rakia* as "firmament" is well-chosen, since the Hebrew idea (Genesis 1:6–8) was that this vault was solid, holding up "the upper waters" and separating them from those which became dry on earth. **3**

כִּרְצוֹנוֹ — ACCORDING TO HIS PLAN: In Hebrew, *kirtzono*—"by His will." This evokes the oft-repeated concept in the prayers (especially on Shabbat, which celebrates creation) of God fashioning the universe according to a preconceived plan. This is sometimes expressed as if the Torah itself were "the plan" which lay before God during creation. At other times, the mystery of creation is treated more obliquely: God simply brought the universe into being "by His word." This is the thought expressed at the beginning of this prayer and discussed in the commentary there. **4**

בּוֹרֵא יוֹם וָלָיְלָה,	1	He creates day and night,
גּוֹלֵל אוֹר מִפְּנֵי חֹשֶׁךְ		rolling away light before darkness and darkness before light.
וְחֹשֶׁךְ מִפְּנֵי אוֹר.	2	He makes a day pass away and brings on night,
וּמַעֲבִיר יוֹם וּמֵבִיא לָיְלָה,		dividing day and night.
וּמַבְדִּיל בֵּין יוֹם וּבֵין לָיְלָה.		As Lord of the hosts of heaven we know Him.
יְיָ צְבָאוֹת שְׁמוֹ.		The living and eternal God will rule forever and ever.
אֵל חַי וְקַיָּם תָּמִיד יִמְלֹךְ		Blessed is the Lord, who has led us to the evening twilight.
עָלֵינוּ לְעוֹלָם וָעֶד.	3	
בָּרוּךְ אַתָּה יְיָ, הַמַּעֲרִיב עֲרָבִים.		

1 יוֹם וָלָיְלָה — DAY AND NIGHT: From earliest times, the alternation of day and night—light and darkness—has had a profound effect on human consciousness. This is expressed poetically in the biblical account of creation. In the primeval chaos, there was "darkness on the face of the deep" until God said: "Let there be light" (Genesis 1:3). The story dwells on the beneficence of this act: "And God saw the light, that it was good; and God divided the light from the darkness. And God called the light Day, and the darkness He called Night" (Genesis 1:4-6). In Jewish thought, Day was to stand mostly for the positive side of life. Awakening in the morning, one gives thanks for being alive. Each day is like a new act of creation by the Almighty. Night, by contrast, stood mostly for danger and fear; yet it has a positive side, too. It is a time for rest and for renewal of strength. It is also a time for meditation, though meditation, too, has its sad side, as expressed by the psalmist (Psalm 77:5-6): "My thoughts went back to times long past; I remembered forgotten years. All night long I was in deep distress; as I lay thinking, my spirit was sunk in despair."

2 וְחֹשֶׁךְ מִפְּנֵי אוֹר — ROLLING AWAY . . . DARKNESS BEFORE LIGHT: In Jewish myth, the terrors of the night may include visits by demons, including Lilith—the she-demon supreme—whose presence meant danger, especially for women in childbirth. But the night, however long, always fades away before the light of day.

3 לְעוֹלָם וָעֶד — FOREVER AND EVER: This familiar phrase *le'olam va'ed* has an interesting origin in Hebrew. Although the word *olam* is usually understood to mean "world," in fact it has this meaning only in later Hebrew. In the Bible, *olam* means "ancient time" or "continuous existence," as in *zechor yemot olam*—"remember the days of old" '(Deuteronomy 32:7). The second half of the phrase (*va'ed*) is also archaic in tone.

This second blessing leading to the *Sh'ma*
is built around God's love for Israel, symbolized in
His giving of the Torah. In the *Sh'ma*, Israel
turns to God in love—"with heart and soul."

AHAVAT OLAM

אַהֲבַת עוֹלָם

אַהֲבַת עוֹלָם בֵּית יִשְׂרָאֵל 1 עַמְּךָ אָהָבְתָּ. 2 תּוֹרָה וּמִצְוֹת, חֻקִּים וּמִשְׁפָּטִים אוֹתָנוּ לִמַּדְתָּ. עַל־כֵּן יְיָ אֱלֹהֵינוּ בְּשָׁכְבֵנוּ וּבְקוּמֵנוּ נָשִׂיחַ בְּחֻקֶּיךָ. וְנִשְׂמַח בְּדִבְרֵי תוֹרָתֶךָ וּבְמִצְוֹתֶיךָ 3 לְעוֹלָם וָעֶד. כִּי הֵם חַיֵּינוּ וְאֹרֶךְ יָמֵינוּ, 4 וּבָהֶם נֶהְגֶּה יוֹמָם וָלָיְלָה. וְאַהֲבָתְךָ אַל תָּסִיר מִמֶּנּוּ לְעוֹלָמִים. בָּרוּךְ אַתָּה יְיָ, אוֹהֵב עַמּוֹ יִשְׂרָאֵל.	Unending is Your love for the 　House of Israel: You have loved 　Your people. Torah and mitzvot, laws and 　precepts You have taught us. Wherefore, O Lord our God, we 　meditate on Your laws when we lie down to sleep and 　when we rise; We rejoice in the words of Your 　Torah and commandments 　forever and ever, for they are 　our life and measure of our 　days; we meditate on them day 　and night. May You never take Your love 　away from us. Blessed is the Lord, who loves His 　people Israel.

אַהֲבַת עוֹלָם — UNENDING IS YOUR LOVE: The Jewish people came into existence when they received, through Revelation, a pattern of conduct which gave
meaning to human existence. The Torah is an expression of God's love.

עַמְּךָ — YOUR PEOPLE: This takes us back to *am segullah*—God's "treasured
people"—discussed earlier (p. 20). Jews always believed not only that God had
"chosen" *them,* but also, in a sense, that they had chosen God. The Torah had been
offered to all nations, but the ancient Hebrews had accepted it.

וְנִשְׂמַח בְּדִבְרֵי תוֹרָתֶךָ — WE REJOICE IN THE WORDS OF YOUR TORAH: For all
the tears of Jewish history, Judaism is a religion of joy. The pride in being Jewish is
more than a reflection of good fellowship; it has given every Jew a sense of
fulfilling God's purpose for mankind.

כִּי הֵם חַיֵּינוּ — FOR THEY ARE OUR LIFE: This brings to mind a saying of the
famous *ḥasid* Rabbi Levi Isaac of Berdichev (1740-1810): "In every action, a man
must regard his body as the Holy of Holies, a part of the supreme power on earth
which is part of the manifestation of the Deity. The brain of man is like unto the
Ark and the two Tables of the Covenant. Whenever a man lifts his hands to do a
deed, let him consider his hands the messengers of God."

When we recite the *Sh'ma* we unite ourselves with the most
abiding element in our religion. The *Sh'ma* is the first affirmation we
learn as children. We are aware of it every day of
our lives as the signal of our existence as Jews. It is our
ultimate affirmation—our last words—as life ends.

SH'MA

שְׁמַע

Deuteronomy 6:4

שְׁמַע יִשְׂרָאֵל יְיָ אֱלֹהֵינוּ 1
יְיָ אֶחָד. 2

Hear, O Israel: The Lord is our God,
the Lord is One.

בָּרוּךְ שֵׁם כְּבוֹד מַלְכוּתוֹ לְעוֹלָם וָעֶד. 3

Blessed is His name; the glory of His
kingdom is eternal.

Sh'ma yisra'el, adonai eloheinu, adonai eḥad.

Baruch shem kevod malchuto le'olam va'ed.

THE SH'MA: The rabbis never tired of talking about how to express the immediacy of the *Sh'ma* to us. It is not enough, said one rabbi, to recite it as part of one's ordinary Bible reading (*Mishnah Berachot* 2:3). It has to be recited separately with intense application, and with every letter pronounced distinctly. Some prayers (e.g., the *Tefillah*) require a formal gathering; the *Sh'ma* is different. Whatever one is doing when the time of day comes to recite the *Sh'ma,* one breaks off for this direct expression of faith. "A workman may recite the *Sh'ma* at the top of a tree, or on a pile of stones during a building job" (*Mishnah Berachot* 2:4).

1   שְׁמַע יִשְׂרָאֵל — HEAR, O ISRAEL: We hear in these magic words the voice of Moses who first spoke them (Deuteronomy 6:4). The setting was intensely dramatic. After forty years of wandering, the Israelites were assembled on the borders of the Promised Land. Moses would never enter it, but his task had been achieved. The book of Deuteronomy is his passionate account of the faith they must live by. He takes them through the dramas of the past, meaningful only if the people of Israel rivet their hopes on the God who has revealed Himself to them. In the affirmation and its succeeding verses, he immortalizes Israel's faith.

2   יְיָ אֶחָד — THE LORD IS ONE: What is the real meaning of *eḥad*—"one"? The ancient Hebrews went far beyond a faith in *one* God as opposed to the pagan worship of *many* gods. The unity of God is not numerical but total. It embraces everything. It brings the infinite into our lives. In reciting the *Sh'ma,* a Jew of mystic leanings will pronounce the word *eḥad* slowly and deliberately, unwilling to let it end, seeking through this word to reach out to the Lord whose inexpressible power established and sustains the universe.

3   שֵׁם — HIS NAME: The name of God that appears in the Bible—written with the letters י, ה, ו, and ה—was too holy to be pronounced except by the High Priest in the Holy of Holies, the inner sanctuary of the Temple, on Yom Kippur, the Day of Atonement. The ordinary Jew touches God's majesty by speaking of Him as *Hashem*—"The Name."

29

Deuteronomy 6:5–9		

וְאָהַבְתָּ אֵת יְיָ אֱלֹהֶיךָ
בְּכָל־לְבָבְךָ וּבְכָל־נַפְשְׁךָ
וּבְכָל־מְאֹדֶךָ.
וְהָיוּ הַדְּבָרִים הָאֵלֶּה אֲשֶׁר אָנֹכִי
מְצַוְּךָ הַיּוֹם עַל לְבָבֶךָ.
וְשִׁנַּנְתָּם לְבָנֶיךָ וְדִבַּרְתָּ בָּם
בְּשִׁבְתְּךָ בְּבֵיתֶךָ
וּבְלֶכְתְּךָ בַדֶּרֶךְ
וּבְשָׁכְבְּךָ וּבְקוּמֶךָ.

1,2

3

4

Love the Lord your God with all
   your heart, with all your soul,
   with all your might.
Lay these words, which I
   command you this day, upon
   your heart.
Teach them diligently to your
   children, and talk of them when
   you sit in your home,
when you are on the way, when
   you lie down, and when you
   rise.

Ve'ahavta et adonai elohecha bechol levavcha uvchol
nafshecha uvchol me'odecha. Vehayu hadevarim ha'eleh
asher anochi metzavcha hayom al levavecha. Veshinantam
levanecha v'dibarta bam beshivtecha beveitecha uvlechtecha
vaderech uvshochbecha uvkumecha.

בְּכָל־לְבָבְךָ — WITH ALL YOUR HEART: This expresses the meaning of prayer in Judaism. The Mishnah says: "If one makes prayer a fixed task, it is no supplication." One must find a way of "directing one's heart toward God." The Gemara expands this (Babylonian Talmud, *Berachot* 29b): "One must be able to add something of oneself to the words." **1**

וּבְכָל־נַפְשְׁךָ — WITH ALL YOUR SOUL: Over the centuries, Jews have found different ways to express passionate love for God in an intense reading of the *Sh'ma*. All prayer—and especially the *Sh'ma*—had to be recited with *kavvanah* ("devotion"). Kabbalists believed that the feeling aroused in a proper recital could lead to the restoration (*tikkun*) of the harmony of the universe. For the Ḥasidim, *kavvanah* came to mean attachment (*devekut*) to God through "enthusiasm." They would move their bodies wildly and shout in ecstasy. For others (e.g., the followers of the Vilna Gaon), devotion to God was expressed not with tumultuous enthusiasm but gently, from the depths of the heart. **2**

וְשִׁנַּנְתָּם לְבָנֶיךָ — TEACH THEM DILIGENTLY TO YOUR CHILDREN: The Hebrew word *ve-shinnantam* is sharp and graphic, from the root *shinnen*, which means "to prick"—to get inside the child's mind. **3**

וּבְלֶכְתְּךָ בַדֶּרֶךְ — WHEN YOU ARE ON THE WAY: The literal translation is "when you walk on the way." Significantly, these "commands" are all in the singular, addressed to each individual Jew. The famous opening command ("Hear, O Israel") is addressed to Israel as a whole: "The Lord *our* God." **4**

30

וּקְשַׁרְתָּם לְאוֹת עַל יָדֶךָ 1
וְהָיוּ לְטֹטָפֹת בֵּין עֵינֶיךָ.
וּכְתַבְתָּם עַל מְזֻזוֹת בֵּיתֶךָ 2,3
וּבִשְׁעָרֶיךָ.

Bind them as a sign upon your arm,
    and as symbols before your
    eyes.
Inscribe them on the doorposts of
    your home and on your gates.

Ukshartam le'ot al yadecha, vehayu letotafot bein einecha.
Uchtavtam al mezuzot beitecha uvish'arecha.

---

1   וּקְשַׁרְתָּם לְאוֹת עַל יָדֶךָ — BIND THEM AS A SIGN UPON YOUR ARM: This is the origin of *tefillin,* small boxes (containing these and other verses) bound by straps on the arm and forehead for the morning recital of prayers. *Tefillah* means "prayer," and it is generally assumed that this is the origin of the word *tefillin.* Therefore, the usual English translation of *tefillin,* "phylactery," from the Greek word meaning "amulet," is incorrect. In his commentary on the prayerbook, the English scholar Israel Abrahams explained, in agreement with Maimonides (see below), that the word "amulet" gives the wrong idea. These central verses of the Jewish faith are included in a "prayer-box" (as also in the *mezuzah* on the doorpost) not "for luck," but to bring home the basic teachings they express. "The *Sh'ma* enshrines the fundamental dogma (Monotheism), the fundamental duty (Love), the fundamental discipline (Study of the Law), and the fundamental method (union of Letter and Spirit in the Jewish religion.)"

2   עַל מְזֻזוֹת — ON THE DOORPOSTS: The Hebrew word for "doorpost" is *mezuzah.* By transference, the word came to apply not to the doorpost itself but to the small case affixed to the doorpost; contained within the case are the two passages in the Torah (Deuteronomy 6:4–9 and 11:13–21) laying down the ordinance for fixing the *mezuzah.* A *mezuzah* parchment containing the second Deuteronomy passage was found at Qumran among the Dead Sea Scrolls, going back to Temple times.

3   בֵּיתֶךָ — YOUR HOUSE: The appearance of a *mezuzah* on the doorpost of a house or room has always generated a great feeling of kinship among Jews. Some have even regarded it as a lucky charm, and have added kabbalistic names and symbols, or the *magen david* ("Shield of David") to the Bible passages. The great medieval scholar Maimonides (1135–1204), a rationalist by temperament, denounced those who thought that a *mezuzah* had some kind of protective effect. "With their foolish hearts," he wrote, "they turn a commandment whose purpose is to emphasize the love of God into an amulet."

Deuteronomy 11:13–21

וְהָיָה אִם שָׁמֹעַ תִּשְׁמְעוּ אֶל
מִצְוֹתַי אֲשֶׁר אָנֹכִי מְצַוֶּה
אֶתְכֶם הַיּוֹם
לְאַהֲבָה אֶת־יְיָ אֱלֹהֵיכֶם וּלְעָבְדוֹ
בְּכָל־לְבַבְכֶם וּבְכָל־נַפְשְׁכֶם.
וְנָתַתִּי מְטַר אַרְצְכֶם בְּעִתּוֹ
יוֹרֶה וּמַלְקוֹשׁ,
וְאָסַפְתָּ דְגָנֶךָ וְתִירֹשְׁךָ וְיִצְהָרֶךָ.
וְנָתַתִּי עֵשֶׂב בְּשָׂדְךָ לִבְהֶמְתֶּךָ,
וְאָכַלְתָּ וְשָׂבָעְתָּ.

It shall come to pass that if you
  hearken truly to My
  commandments that I command
  you this day,
to love the Lord your God and serve
  Him with all your heart and all
  your soul,
I will give you the rain of your land
  in its season,
the early rain and the late rain,
that you may gather in your corn,
  your wine and your oil.
I will give grass in your field for
  your cattle,
and you shall eat and be satisfied.

מְטַר אַרְצְכֶם בְּעִתּוֹ — THE RAIN OF YOUR LAND IN ITS SEASON: This second **1**
section of the *Sh'ma* begins with one of the many passages in the Bible which
reflect the fact that rain was always uncertain and crucially important for the
agriculture of the Holy Land. The horrors of drought are evoked brilliantly in a
famous passage by Jeremiah (14:2–6): "Judah mourns, her settlements languish,
men are bowed to the ground, and the outcry of Jerusalem rises. . . . Because the
ground is chapped, for there was no rain in the earth; the plowmen are shamed,
they cover their heads. . . . Wild asses stand on the bare heights, sniffing the air
like jackals; their eyes pine because there is no grass."

יוֹרֶה וּמַלְקוֹשׁ — EARLY RAIN AND LATE RAIN: These two Hebrew words are **2**
archaic. *Yoreh* ("early rain")—from a root which means to shoot or throw—takes
place normally from the end of October (after Sukkot, the Feast of Tabernacles) to
the beginning of December. *Malkosh* ("late rain")—a word formed from an obscure
source—refers to the showers of March and April, which end the rainy season.

דְגָנֶךָ וְתִירֹשְׁךָ וְיִצְהָרֶךָ — YOUR CORN, YOUR WINE AND YOUR OIL: These **3**
three basic products—*dagan, tirosh, yitzhar*—frequently appear together to illustrate
the fertility of the Holy Land. Not surprisingly, they are included in God's description for Aaron and his descendants of the enormous bounty to which they will be
entitled for carrying out the Temple services (Numbers 18:12): "I give you all the
choicest of the oil, the choicest of the new wine, and the corn, the first-fruits
which are given to God. . . . Everything in Israel which has been devoted to God
shall be yours."

הִשָּׁמְרוּ לָכֶם פֶּן יִפְתֶּה לְבַבְכֶם
וְסַרְתֶּם וַעֲבַדְתֶּם אֱלֹהִים
אֲחֵרִים וְהִשְׁתַּחֲוִיתֶם לָהֶם.
וְחָרָה אַף יְיָ בָּכֶם וְעָצַר
אֶת־הַשָּׁמַיִם
וְלֹא יִהְיֶה מָטָר, וְהָאֲדָמָה
לֹא תִתֵּן אֶת־יְבוּלָהּ,
וַאֲבַדְתֶּם מְהֵרָה מֵעַל הָאָרֶץ
הַטֹּבָה אֲשֶׁר יְיָ נֹתֵן לָכֶם.

1,2

Take heed lest your heart be
  deceived
and you turn aside to serve other
  gods and worship them.
The Lord's anger will be kindled
  against you:
He will close up the heavens:
there will be no rain; the land will
  not yield its produce
and you will perish quickly from the
  good land which the Lord has
  given you.

1 וְחָרָה אַף יְיָ — THE LORD'S ANGER WILL BE KINDLED: Humanity is free to choose the good life, yet it persists in destroying itself, "turning aside to serve false gods," frustrating the hopes that God has for the world, and thus "angering" Him. Poetically, God comes nearer to humanity when He is talked of in quasi-human terms. The stark anthropomorphisms of the Bible are often mellowed by the rabbis into imaginative tales. In the Talmud, for example, we are told that God actually wears *tefillin* ("prayer boxes"; see p. 31) when He prays. But what does He say in His prayers? "May it be My will that My compassion overcome My anger: that I may deal with My children by My attribute of compassion, and not according to the strict line of justice" (Babylonian Talmud, *Berachot* 7a).

2 וְעָצַר אֶת־הַשָּׁמַיִם — HE WILL CLOSE UP THE HEAVENS: This threat remained vivid in the minds of Jews long after they had dispersed to lands in which rain was sometimes all too frequent. A formal prayer for rain became, for Jews throughout the world, a central feature of the service on Shemini Atzeret, the day marking the conclusion of Sukkot, the Feast of Tabernacles, when the early rain was due. The greatest religious poet of the early Middle Ages, Eleazar Kallir, who is thought to have lived in the Holy Land in the seventh century, composed a number of elaborate *piyyutim* ("prayer poems") on this subject. His works became—and have remained—a regular part of the formal service on Shemini Atzeret. The intensity of the prayer that rain might fall in the Holy Land is shown by the fact that in traditional synagogues—throughout Eastern Europe and elsewhere—the cantor would dress for this service in the same *kittel* ("white robe") that was otherwise only used at Rosh Hashanah and Yom Kippur.

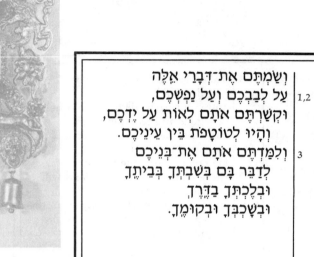

וְשַׂמְתֶּם אֶת־דְּבָרַי אֵלֶּה
עַל לְבַבְכֶם וְעַל נַפְשְׁכֶם,
וּקְשַׁרְתֶּם אֹתָם לְאוֹת עַל יֶדְכֶם,
וְהָיוּ לְטוֹטָפֹת בֵּין עֵינֵיכֶם.
וְלִמַּדְתֶּם אֹתָם אֶת־בְּנֵיכֶם
לְדַבֵּר בָּם בְּשִׁבְתְּךָ בְּבֵיתֶךָ
וּבְלֶכְתְּךָ בַדֶּרֶךְ
וּבְשָׁכְבְּךָ וּבְקוּמֶךָ.

1,2

3

Therefore lay these My words upon
your heart and upon your soul;
bind them as a sign upon your arm
and as symbols before your
eyes.
Teach them to your children
and talk of them when you sit in
your home,
when you are on the way, when you
lie down, and when you rise.

עַל לְבַבְכֶם — UPON YOUR HEART: "Heart" (*lev, levav*) in the Bible is used to denote the seat of the emotions. All feeling and thought are taken as coming from the interior of the body. A favorite way to describe strong feeling is to speak of the stirring of the intestines. Gladness is thought of as located in the kidneys, as well as in the heart. But above all, the heart is taken as the seat of the intellect. To be "wise of heart" means to be intelligent or skillful. One might translate *lev* more accurately, H. L. Ginsberg says, as "mind," with the link here to "teaching the children." 1

וְעַל נַפְשְׁכֶם — UPON YOUR SOUL: In the Bible, the "soul" (*nefesh*) is the essence of the person; body and soul are integrated. In rabbinic times a conception arose of the soul as a separate animating force of the material body. The rabbis used to say that on the eve of Shabbat, God gives man "an extra soul" to enjoy the day. 2

וְלִמַּדְתֶּם אֹתָם אֶת־בְּנֵיכֶם — TEACH THEM TO YOUR CHILDREN: This injunction is the classical source for the emphasis on education which has been so prevalent in Jewish life for endless centuries. In the midrash on the Garden of Eden, says the English scholar Rabbi David Goldstein, "the Tree of Life and the Tree of Knowledge are connected. In the very center of the garden stood the Tree of Life and around it and protecting it, as it were, was the Tree of Knowledge, which was of prodigious size. One would have to travel for 500 years just to circumnavigate the trunk, let alone explore the whole area beneath its branches [*Genesis Rabbah* 15:6]. Did the Tree of Life then somehow grow out of the Tree of Knowledge? Such, it appears, was the view of one commentator on Genesis, Rabbenu Baḥya ben Asher [d. 1340], who wrote that both trees 'formed one tree at the bottom, and branched out into two when they reached a certain height'." 3

וּכְתַבְתָּם עַל מְזוּזוֹת בֵּיתֶךָ
וּבִשְׁעָרֶיךָ.
לְמַעַן יִרְבּוּ יְמֵיכֶם וִימֵי בְנֵיכֶם
עַל הָאֲדָמָה אֲשֶׁר נִשְׁבַּע יְיָ
לַאֲבֹתֵיכֶם לָתֵת לָהֶם
כִּימֵי הַשָּׁמַיִם עַל הָאָרֶץ.

1

Numbers 15:37–41

וַיֹּאמֶר יְיָ אֶל מֹשֶׁה לֵּאמֹר.
דַּבֵּר אֶל בְּנֵי יִשְׂרָאֵל וְאָמַרְתָּ
אֲלֵהֶם וְעָשׂוּ לָהֶם צִיצִת
עַל כַּנְפֵי בִגְדֵיהֶם לְדֹרֹתָם,
וְנָתְנוּ עַל צִיצִת הַכָּנָף
פְּתִיל תְּכֵלֶת.

2

3

Inscribe them on the doorposts of
your home and on your gates,
that your days, and the days of your
children, be multiplied—
as the days of heaven above the
earth—
in the land which the Lord swore
unto your fathers to give to
them.

The Lord said to Moses:
Speak to the children of Israel and
bid them make a tassel—*tzitzit*—
on the corners of their garments
throughout their generations.
They shall put upon the *tzitzit* of
each corner a thread of blue.

---

1   לְמַעַן יִרְבּוּ יְמֵיכֶם — THAT YOUR DAYS . . . BE MULTIPLIED: This second section of the *Sh'ma* has dealt with reward and punishment, depending on how God's
commands are fulfilled. If His people fail, God "will close up the heavens," and His
people will perish. If they obey, their days "will be multiplied." Yet, to the Rabbis,
obedience was spiritualized: "Be not as servants who minister to their master on
the condition of receiving a reward" (Ethics of the Fathers 1:3).

2   צִיצִת עַל כַּנְפֵי בִגְדֵיהֶם — A TASSEL—*tzitzit*—ON THE CORNERS OF THEIR
GARMENTS: This injunction, going back in the Bible to Moses, has become traditional practice, sustained unbroken for more than 3,000 years. In no sense is the
tzitzit worn as an amulet—for luck. The biblical passage gives the true meaning
(Numbers 15:39): "When you look at the *tzitzit*, you will remember all the *mitzvot*
("commandments") of the Lord and perform them." A Jew accepts that life
demands self-discipline, a pattern of conduct expressed in the moral purpose of the
mitzvot. To wear the *tzitzit* brings this home.

3   פְּתִיל תְּכֵלֶת — A THREAD OF BLUE: It is believed that a blue thread was introduced to express the color of the sky, which made the Jew think of "the throne
of glory" (Babylonian Talmud, *Menahot* 43a). When the right dye for this purpose
proved difficult to get, the rabbis of the second century waived this requirement.

וְהָיָה לָכֶם לְצִיצִת וּרְאִיתֶם אֹתוֹ
וּזְכַרְתֶּם אֶת־כָּל־מִצְוֹת יְיָ ‎1
וַעֲשִׂיתֶם אֹתָם,
וְלֹא תָתוּרוּ אַחֲרֵי לְבַבְכֶם
וְאַחֲרֵי עֵינֵיכֶם
אֲשֶׁר אַתֶּם זֹנִים אַחֲרֵיהֶם.
לְמַעַן תִּזְכְּרוּ וַעֲשִׂיתֶם
אֶת־כָּל־מִצְוֹתָי
וִהְיִיתֶם קְדֹשִׁים לֵאלֹהֵיכֶם. ‎2
אֲנִי יְיָ אֱלֹהֵיכֶם אֲשֶׁר הוֹצֵאתִי
אֶתְכֶם מֵאֶרֶץ מִצְרַיִם
לִהְיוֹת לָכֶם לֵאלֹהִים,
אֲנִי יְיָ אֱלֹהֵיכֶם.
אֱמֶת. ‎3

When you look at the *tzitzit*,
 you will remember all the
 commandments—*mitzvot*—of the
 Lord and perform them,
So you will not act impulsively
 and casually and thus be led
 astray.
You are to remember and carry out
 all My *mitzvot*, and be holy to
 your God.
For I am the Lord your God,
 who brought you out of the
 land of Egypt to be your God.
I am the Lord your God.

Emet—The Truth.

וּזְכַרְתֶּם — YOU WILL REMEMBER: As a reminder of the *mitzvot*, the *tzitzit* has the same function as the *tefillin* and the *mezuzah*, instituted in the *Sh'ma* passages. But the tzitzit is more intimate and continuous in its role. Wherever he is, a Jew carries the *tzitzit* with him all day. His feeling of being a Jew, and what is involved in it, never leaves him. It became the custom to wear the *tzitzit* on the four corners of a *tallit katan*, a rectangular garment of white cotton, linen, or wool.

וִהְיִיתֶם קְדֹשִׁים לֵאלֹהֵיכֶם — AND BE HOLY TO YOUR GOD: This echoes the famous injunction of Leviticus (19:2), repeated many times in various forms: "You shall be holy, for I the Lord your God am holy." On one level, the holiness of the Hebrew people was to be expressed in the strict observance by priests and ordinary people of ethical rules and rituals covering sacrifices, feast days, and personal cleanliness as set out in chapters known as "the Holiness Code" (Leviticus 17–26). On another, it was a totally spiritual concept, illustrating, as Rabbi Baruch Levine has said, how the Bible radically refashioned notions of the sacred in the religions of the Near East: "In primitive Semitic religions, the holy is considered an intrinsic, impersonal, neutral quality inherent in objects, persons, rites and sites. . . . In biblical religion, on the contrary, holiness expresses the very nature of God, and it is He who is its ultimate source and is denominated as the Holy One."

אֱמֶת — TRUE: Traditionally, this first word of the following blessing is tacked onto the end of the *Sh'ma*, as if the worshipers feel obliged, after the recital of its passages, to utter this word, as expressing the depth of their feeling about the *Sh'ma*.

This first blessing after the *Sh'ma*
deals with Israel as a nation and talks of
God's redemptive power—*ge'ulah.*

GE'ULAH

גְּאֻלָה

אֱמֶת וֶאֱמוּנָה כָּל־זֹאת	1	True and trustworthy is all this, and it is established with us
וְקַיָּם עָלֵינוּ		That He is the Lord our God, incomparable,
כִּי הוּא יְיָ אֱלֹהֵינוּ וְאֵין זוּלָתוֹ,		And we are His people Israel.
וַאֲנַחְנוּ יִשְׂרָאֵל עַמּוֹ.		He has delivered us from the power of kings,
הַפּוֹדֵנוּ מִיַּד מְלָכִים,	2	*Our* King has rescued us from the grasp of tyrants.
מַלְכֵּנוּ הַגֹּאֲלֵנוּ מִכַּף		
כָּל־הֶעָרִיצִים.		

REDEEMER OF ISRAEL: This prayer brings together biblical passages, as will be seen, to establish the role of God in Jewish history. The God of creation is the God of our *ge'ulah* ("redemption"). He has saved us from oppression, "and from the grasp of tyrants." The key redemption, symbol of all the deliverances which were to follow, was the Exodus, celebrated in Moses's song of triumph (Exodus 15), when the waters of the *yam suf* ("Sea of Reeds") parted and the Hebrews passed over on dry land. This event is mentioned repeatedly in the prayer, and verses are drawn from Moses's song.

1 אֱמֶת וֶאֱמוּנָה — TRUE AND TRUSTWORTHY: This prayer—similar to one recited after the *Sh'ma* in the morning service—has its origin at least as far back as the second century, according to a passage in the Babylonian Talmud (*Berachot* 12a). The Talmud also explains an interesting change from the morning service: the addition of the word *emunah* ("trustworthy"). This addition was apparently made because this blessing is an evening prayer in order to reflect the opening of Psalm 92: "It is good to give thanks to God . . . to declare your constancy (*emunatecha*) at night."

2 מִיַּד מְלָכִים — FROM THE POWER OF KINGS: The enemy kings who come to mind include Pharaoh, Sihon, Og, and Amalek (legendary enemies in the forty-year wanderings in the wilderness), followed by Nebuchadnezzar, who destroyed the First Temple, and the Roman emperors who accomplished the final destruction of the Second. In rabbinic writings, the emperor Hadrian, who defeated Bar Kochba and outlawed Bible teaching, was always mentioned with a curse: "Hadrian, may his bones be crushed!" This prayer reminds us of some famous acts of *ge'ulah* ("redemption"): the victory over Antiochus (celebrated on Ḥanukkah) and the victory over Haman (celebrated on Purim).

הָאֵל הַנִּפְרָע לָנוּ מִצָּרֵינוּ,
וְהַמְשַׁלֵּם גְּמוּל לְכָל־אוֹיְבֵי
נַפְשֵׁנוּ.
הָעֹשֶׂה גְדֹלוֹת עַד־אֵין חֵקֶר,
וְנִפְלָאוֹת עַד אֵין מִסְפָּר.
הַשָּׂם נַפְשֵׁנוּ בַּחַיִּים, |1
וְלֹא נָתַן לַמּוֹט רַגְלֵינוּ. |2
הַמַּדְרִיכֵנוּ עַל בָּמוֹת אוֹיְבֵינוּ, |3
וַיָּרֶם קַרְנֵנוּ עַל כָּל־שׂוֹנְאֵינוּ. |4

He has meted out punishment to
our adversaries,
And requited the enmities we have
suffered.
He has done marvels beyond
conception, wonders without
number.
He has kept us alive, and never
suffered our feet to slip.
He has let us tread down the high
places of our enemies,
And lifted our heads high over all
who hate us.

הַשָּׂם נַפְשֵׁנוּ בַּחַיִּים — "HE HAS KEPT US ALIVE": A direct quote from Psalm 66:9. |1
Literally: "He has kept our (soul) *nefesh* in life." *Nefesh,* as noted above (p. 34), refers
to one's whole existence, not merely to "the soul" in a modern sense.

וְלֹא נָתַן לַמּוֹט רַגְלֵנוּ — "NEVER SUFFERED OUR FOOT TO SLIP": A quote from |2
Psalm 121:3, a most popular psalm—"I will lift up mine eyes unto the hills. . . ."

הַמַּדְרִיכֵנוּ עַל בָּמוֹת אוֹיְבֵינוּ — "HE HAS LET US TREAD DOWN THE HIGH |3
PLACES OF OUR ENEMIES": This again is a direct quote from the Bible
(Deuteronomy 33:29), but one with a multiple meaning which throws light on
how the Jews drew on the Bible. In the original, the verse appears as archaic
poetry, often difficult to understand. It is from Moses' final Blessing, in which he
tells his followers, "You will tread upon the high places (*bamot*) of your enemies." In
biblical terminology, *bamot* were the "high places" of pagan idolatry which the true
followers of God were to "tread down." This, undoubtedly, is how the original
composers of this prayer would have understood the words they drew on. Modern
translators take *bamot* to mean something different in the Deuteronomy passage.
The 1967 translation by the Jewish Publication Society of America gives the verse
as: "You shall tread on their backs." The New English Bible (1970) says: "You shall
trample their bodies underfoot."

וַיָּרֶם קַרְנֵנוּ — LIFTED OUR HEAD HIGH: The Hebrew words *va-yarem karnenu* |4
mean literally: "He has lifted our horn (*keren*)." In ancient Hebrew poetry, the horn
is a symbol of strength of an animal. For God to "lift up the horn of Israel" is to let
Israel stand proudly, head high.

הֶעָשָׂה לָנוּ נִסִּים וּנְקָמָה בְּפַרְעֹה,	1,2	He did miracles for us, and vengeance against Pharaoh, signs and wonders in the land of Egypt.
אוֹתוֹת וּמוֹפְתִים בְּאַדְמַת	3	
בְּנֵי חָם.		

1   הֶעָשָׂה לָנוּ נִסִּים — HE DID MIRACLES FOR US: The prayer now begins to deal slowly and happily with the Exodus from Egypt, the supreme occasion in Israel's history, which established for all time that God had taken this people under His care and that they were to become a nation in their own land, enjoying "everlasting freedom." When Jews gather to pray, they are ready to forget for a time the many disasters which are a part of their history. The miracle of Jewish survival overshadows miseries and tragedies. This mood is paralleled exactly by the spirit at the Passover Seder when the celebrants begin the recital of the song *Dayyenu* ("We would have been satisfied"). In that spirit, one lists the bounties, and lingers over them. The miseries and tragedies are ignored. It is the positive side of Jewish life that matters, and the Exodus is its symbol. Throughout the Bible, everything positive is defined in terms of our delivery from slavery in Egypt, that far-off event which remained central in significance in the minds of Jews. Yet as detailed as the story is, no one would ever imagine that the deliverance had been the result of natural causes. It was inexplicable except in terms of the bounty of God, the miracles He did for us.

2   וּנְקָמָה בְּפַרְעֹה — VENGEANCE AGAINST PHARAOH: The Song of Moses (Exodus 15:1-19), celebrating the deliverance at the "Red Sea" (more correctly, "the Sea of Reeds") expresses a good deal of glee at the fate of Pharaoh. The poetry—extremely ancient in style—is vivid with excitement: "The enemy said: I will pursue, I will overtake, I will divide the spoil; my lust shall be satisfied upon them; I will draw my sword, my hand shall destroy them. Thou didst blow with thy wind, the sea covered them; they sank as lead in the mighty waters." The brief Song of Miriam, which is appended to the song of her brother and is thought to be perhaps the oldest strand of the Bible text, is even more graphic and pithy. Every Jew recalls her refrain as she takes up her timbrel and gathers the women around her in a wild dance of triumph: "Sing ye to the Lord, for He has triumphed gloriously: horse and rider has He thrown into the sea."

3   בְּאַדְמַת בְּנֵי חָם — IN THE LAND OF EGYPT: The literal meaning of the Hebrew is: "In the land of the children of Ham." Ham was the second son of Noah. In late parts of the book of Psalms the name is used—though no one knows why—as a collective name for Egyptians.

הַמַּכֶּה בְעֶבְרָתוֹ כָּל־בְּכוֹרֵי מִצְרַיִם,	1,2	He smote with His right arm all the firstborn of Egypt,
וַיּוֹצֵא אֶת־עַמּוֹ יִשְׂרָאֵל מִתּוֹכָם לְחֵרוּת עוֹלָם.		and brought out His people Israel to everlasting freedom.
הַמַּעֲבִיר בָּנָיו בֵּין גִּזְרֵי יַם סוּף,	3	He made His children pass between the divisions of the Sea of Reeds,
אֶת־רוֹדְפֵיהֶם וְאֶת־שׂוֹנְאֵיהֶם בִּתְהוֹמוֹת טִבַּע.		but sank their pursuers and their enemies in the depths.

הַמַּכֶּה בְעֶבְרָתוֹ — HE SMOTE WITH HIS RIGHT ARM: The Rabbis loved to exult in the triumph over Egypt, yet they went out of their way to warn against too great a desire for vengeance. The Talmud tells us that when the angels in heaven saw the Egyptians drowning in the Sea of Reeds, they burst into song, whereupon God stopped them, saying: "They are my creatures who are drowning. How dare you sing?" (Babylonian Talmud, *Sanhedrin* 39b). **1**

כָּל־בְּכוֹרֵי מִצְרַיִם — ALL THE FIRSTBORN OF EGYPT: The tenth plague, in which all the firstborn males of Egypt were slain by God's intervention and the Jewish firstborn were spared (Exodus 11:5, 12:12), gives a mythic significance to the biblical requirement that the male firstborn of man and beast be devoted to God: "All the firstborn are Mine, for on the day that I smote all the firstborn in the land of Egypt, I hallowed unto Me all the firstborn in Israel, both man and beast. Mine shall they be. I am the Lord" (Numbers 3:13). Going back to primitive times, the male firstborn had always had a special cultic significance. Among ancient peoples who practiced human sacrifice, the firstborn male was considered the most acceptable to the gods. (We hear in 2 Kings 3:27 of Mesha, king of Moab, sacrificing his firstborn son in the hope of averting a military defeat.) As Hebrew life developed, a system emerged in which the priests organized a class of assistants—the Levites—who took the place of the firstborn in the service of God. This exchange is described in Num. 3:12–13. **2**

יַם סוּף — THE SEA OF REEDS: The Hebrew is *yam suf*, and *suf* means "reeds" or "rushes." Many biblical references to *yam suf* (e.g., in Exodus 23:31) clearly mean the Red Sea as we now know it, but most scholars today accept that the stretch of water which became dry for a time in the story of the Exodus, and thus allowed the Hebrews to escape their Egyptian pursuers, must have been a shallow "lake of rushes"—one of the lagoons on the shores of the Mediterranean. **3**

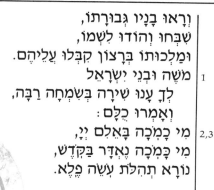

וְרָאוּ בָנָיו גְּבוּרָתוֹ,
שִׁבְּחוּ וְהוֹדוּ לִשְׁמוֹ,
וּמַלְכוּתוֹ בְּרָצוֹן קִבְּלוּ עֲלֵיהֶם.
מֹשֶׁה וּבְנֵי יִשְׂרָאֵל 1
לְךָ עָנוּ שִׁירָה בְּשִׂמְחָה רַבָּה,
וְאָמְרוּ כֻלָּם :
מִי כָמֹכָה בָּאֵלִם יְיָ, 2,3
מִי כָּמֹכָה נֶאְדָּר בַּקֹּדֶשׁ,
נוֹרָא תְהִלֹּת עֹשֵׂה פֶלֶא.

When His children witnessed His
   power, they extolled and gave
   thanks to His name:
Freely they acclaimed Him King.
Moses and the children of Israel
   sang a song to God in great joy,
   saying:
Who is like unto You, O Lord,
   among the mighty ones?
Who is like unto You, majestic in
   holiness, awesome in splendor,
   doing wonders?

1   מֹשֶׁה וּבְנֵי יִשְׂרָאֵל — MOSES AND THE CHILDREN OF ISRAEL: In folk memory, Moses is undoubtedly the greatest of all leaders, unique in his closeness to God, with whom he spoke "face to face" (Exodus 33:11). Maimonides proclaimed this uniqueness of Moses in the seventh of his Thirteen Principles of Faith, which was later echoed in in the *Yigdal* hymn (p. 84): "No prophet has arisen in Israel like Moses—prophet and close to God's radiance." But Jewish tradition firmly conveys that Moses was never "divine." The Passover Haggadah does not even mention him, so as to ascribe the Exodus solely to God.

2   מִי כָמֹכָה — WHO IS LIKE UNTO YOU: This shout of triumph from the Song of Moses (Exodus 15:11) has tremendous verve in Hebrew and is perennially popular. It is translated here with the archaic "unto you" to match the old Hebrew style of spelling *chamokhah*. The initials of the complete phrase מִי כָמֹכָה בָּאֵלִם יְיָ were thought by some to have been combined to form the word "Maccabee" (מַכַּבִּי). According to this view, The hero Judah Maccabee took the phrase from the Song of Moses as his war cry. (Modern scholars doubt this, but have no satisfactory alternative to offer for the derivation of the name Maccabee).

3   בָּאֵלִם — AMONG THE MIGHTY ONES: *Elim* in Hebrew literally means "the gods." *El* was the name of the supreme god of the Canaanites, and was also used for lesser gods. If the Song of Moses goes back to his time—perhaps the thirteenth century B.C.E.—it would be natural to think of the Israelite God as superior to others, though according to the teachings of Moses He was not "superior" but unique, the sole power in the universe.

41

מַלְכוּתְךָ רָאוּ בָנֶיךָ בּוֹקֵעַ יָם לִפְנֵי מֹשֶׁה.	Your children saw Your sovereign power, as You cleft the sea before Moses.
זֶה אֵלִי עָנוּ וְאָמְרוּ:	This is my God, they exclaimed, saying:
יְיָ יִמְלֹךְ לְעֹלָם וָעֶד.	The Lord shall reign forever and ever.
וְנֶאֱמַר:	It is as the Bible says: The Lord has freed Jacob,
כִּי פָדָה יְיָ אֶת־יַעֲקֹב, וּגְאָלוֹ מִיַּד חָזָק מִמֶּנּוּ.	And redeemed him from the hand of one who was stronger than he.
בָּרוּךְ אַתָּה יְיָ, גָּאַל יִשְׂרָאֵל.	Be blessed, O Lord, Redeemer of Israel.

בּוֹקֵעַ יָם לִפְנֵי מֹשֶׁה — YOU CLEFT THE SEA BEFORE MOSES: In the biblical passage describing this event (Exodus 14), it seems at first as if Moses himself will cleave the Sea of Reeds, since God says to him: "Lift up thy rod . . . and divide the sea" (Exodus 14:10). But in verse 21 it becomes quite clear that the miracle has been wrought by God: "And Moses stretched out his hand over the sea, and the Lord caused the sea to go back . . . all that night, and made the sea dry land." As the Bible scholar Moshe Greenberg writes: "No room is left for regarding Moses as a magician, aggrandizing himself through natural powers or occult arts."

יְיָ יִמְלֹךְ — THE LORD SHALL REIGN: This is the dramatic climax of the Song of Moses (Exodus 15:18). It is easy to imagine the people of Israel singing it "with great joy." How well it moves into the concluding blessing: "Be blessed, O Lord, Redeemer of Israel."

גָּאַל יִשְׂרָאֵל — REDEEMER OF ISRAEL: The Hebrew word ga'al ("redeem") has a deeper meaning than merely "save." The Hebrew root meant originally to give help as a kinsman. One sees this in the book of Ruth (2:20), where Naomi tells Ruth that Boaz, on whose farm she gleaned, is "one of our kinsmen" (migo'alenu) (Ruth 2:20). Similarly, the word go'el is applied to the kinsman who helps a widow. Poetically, in this prayer God as a Redeemer is helping His people as a kinsman. The full meaning emerges in the famous passage in the book of Job: "I know that my Redeemer lives," where go'ali means "my defender," "my vindicator" (Job 19:25).

The preceding blessing dealt with Israel
as a people. By contrast, this beautiful prayer is
intensely personal. Hashkivenu is the second
prayer to follow the *Sh'ma*, completing the cycle
ordained by Mishnaic injunction (p. 24).

HASHKIVENU

הַשְׁכִּיבֵנוּ

הַשְׁכִּיבֵנוּ יְיָ אֱלֹהֵינוּ לְשָׁלוֹם,	1
וְהַעֲמִידֵנוּ מַלְכֵּנוּ לְחַיִּים,	
וּפְרוֹשׂ עָלֵינוּ סֻכַּת שְׁלוֹמֶךָ,	2
וְתַקְּנֵנוּ בְּעֵצָה טוֹבָה מִלְּפָנֶיךָ,	
וְהוֹשִׁיעֵנוּ לְמַעַן שְׁמֶךָ.	
וְהָגֵן בַּעֲדֵנוּ, וְהָסֵר מֵעָלֵינוּ	3
אוֹיֵב, דֶּבֶר, וְחֶרֶב,	
וְרָעָב, וְיָגוֹן.	
וְהָסֵר שָׂטָן מִלְּפָנֵינוּ וּמֵאַחֲרֵינוּ,	
וּבְצֵל כְּנָפֶיךָ תַּסְתִּירֵנוּ.	
כִּי אֵל שׁוֹמְרֵנוּ וּמַצִּילֵנוּ אָתָּה,	
כִּי אֵל מֶלֶךְ חַנּוּן וְרַחוּם אָתָּה.	4

Let us lie down, O Lord our God,
to peace;
Let us rise, O our King, to life.
Spread over us the tabernacle of
Your peace,
Direct us through Your own good
counsel,
Save us in the spirit of Your name.
Be a shield around us, keeping at a
distance enmity, disease and
war, hunger and anguish.
Keep the Adversary distant,
before and behind us,
Shelter us in the shadow of Your
wings.
For You are our guardian and
deliverer,
A gracious and merciful King.

1   הַשְׁכִּיבֵנוּ — LET US LIE DOWN: As we lie down or lie awake at night, we grope for reassurance that can strengthen us with hope and courage for the day that lies ahead. A *hashkivenu* prayer goes back to talmudic times. The Hebrew is gentle and meditative, with poetry that lies sweetly in the mind.

2   סֻכַּת שְׁלוֹמֶךָ — THE TABERNACLE OF YOUR PEACE: In Hebrew, "the *sukkah* of Your peace," conveying a delightful echo of the *sukkah* we live in so happily during Sukkot, the Feast of Tabernacles.

3   וְהָגֵן — BE A SHIELD: After the turmoil of the day, we long for a refreshing sleep that will restore within us true peace of mind. But often at night, with the routine activities of the day over, the specters of strife and illness begin to rise. With the calm words of *hashkivenu,* we turn away from our own troubles to the grace that God's protection can afford.

4   חַנּוּן וְרַחוּם — GRACIOUS AND MERCIFUL: In the whole of this meditation, there is no claim of self-justification, no confession of fault or sin, no repentance. What does emerge is humility. Alone with ourselves, we know that we are in God's hands. If we are to sleep and to "rise to life" on the morrow, it will be by His mercy. When we have touched bottom in humility, we see at last the marvel of human existence. In the spirit of the eighth Psalm—"what is man that You are mindful of him?"—we move from fear into celebration: "You have made him little less than divine . . . laying the world at his feet" (Psalm 8:5–6).

וּשְׁמֹר צֵאתֵנוּ וּבוֹאֵנוּ לְחַיִּים	1	Guard us in our coming and going, for life and peace,
וּלְשָׁלוֹם		Now and forever.
מֵעַתָּה וְעַד עוֹלָם,		Spread over us the shelter of Your peace.
וּפְרוֹשׂ עָלֵינוּ סֻכַּת שְׁלוֹמֶךָ.		Be blessed, O Lord, who spreads the shelter of peace
בָּרוּךְ אַתָּה יְיָ,		Over us, and over His people Israel, and over Jerusalem.
הַפּוֹרֵשׂ סֻכַּת שָׁלוֹם		
עָלֵינוּ וְעַל כָּל־עַמּוֹ יִשְׂרָאֵל	2	
וְעַל יְרוּשָׁלָיִם.		

וּשְׁמֹר צֵאתֵנוּ וּבוֹאֵנוּ — GUARD US IN OUR COMING AND GOING: Literally, the Hebrew phrase means "in our going out and coming in." This part of the prayer seems to pick up the thought of the earlier phrase, in which we ask for security against *satan*—"Satan, the adversary," hoping that he will be kept far away "from before and behind us." It is quite understandable that these kinds of fears, linked to myths and legends, would arise in us at night, either half-asleep or in nightmares. Also a danger in the nighttime was Lilith, the female-demon who was thought to roam the world at night, populating the world with her evil offspring, and bringing danger to all, especially to pregnant women. It is an interesting testament to the purity of the biblical tradition that we only hear of myths like that of Lilith long after the period covered by the basic Bible writings.

The same is true of the tales of Satan, "the adversary." The most familiar Bible reference is in Job (chapters 1–2) where Satan has a mischievous—but not necessarily evil—role in God's celestial court in questioning the supposed integrity of this wholly good man Job. Satan suggests that God test Job's integrity by heaping disasters upon him. Satan becomes more prominent as an idea of evil in the Apocrypha, though still not fully personalized in the manner which has entered the Western tradition, largely through Christianity, but also in Jewish legend.

וְעַל כָּל־עַמּוֹ יִשְׂרָאֵל וְעַל יְרוּשָׁלָיִם — AND OVER HIS PEOPLE ISRAEL AND OVER JERUSALEM: This simple phrase expresses the unbreakable link in Jewish feeling which has been potent in all the centuries of the Diaspora. Jerusalem was "the joy of the whole world," it was "the city which men call the perfection of beauty" (Lamentations 2:15). In exile in Babylon, "we sat and wept when we remembered Zion" (Psalm 137:1). When the city finally fell before the Romans in 70 C.E., the hope of a restoration became the dominant feeling: "Next Year in Jerusalem."

Shabbat is more than a day of rest. We see
it here as a part of the "everlasting
Covenant"—a special bond—between
God and the Jewish people.

VESHAMERU

וְשָׁמְרוּ

Exodus 31:16-17

וְשָׁמְרוּ בְנֵי יִשְׂרָאֵל אֶת־הַשַּׁבָּת, | 1,2 | And the children of Israel shall keep the Sabbath,

לַעֲשׂוֹת אֶת־הַשַּׁבָּת לְדֹרֹתָם | 3,4 | observing the Sabbath throughout their generations.

Veshameru venei yisra'el et hashabbat,
la'asot et hashabbat ledorotam

---

1   וְשָׁמְרוּ — SHALL KEEP: The traditional phrase "keep the Sabbath," in the sense of observing it, conveys only part of the meaning of the Hebrew word *veshameru*. The Hebrew root *shamar* also means "guard" or "preserve," which is how *veshameru* sounds to the ear.

2   הַשַּׁבָּת — THE SABBATH: The word *shabbat* means "rest" or "cessation." The full phrase in the Bible is *yom ha-shabbat*—"the day of rest," from which *shabbat* itself came to denote the day. The origin of Shabbat is related, in the first two chapters of the book of Genesis, to God having rested on the seventh day of creation. But the status of that day as a *ritual* day of rest for the Jewish people does not appear in the Bible until the Israelites were collecting the manna daily in the wilderness. On Friday they found double portions of manna; Moses explained that they were to collect twice as much on Friday because on the following day there would be none—it would be "a rest day (*shabbaton*), a holy rest (*shabbat kodesh*) to God" (Exodus 16: 22-27). The next reference to the observance or preservation of Shabbat is in the fourth of the Ten Commandments (Exodus 20:8-11); no work was to be done on Shabbat because God Himself had rested on the seventh day. From then on, Shabbat is seen as central to Israel's faith "throughout their generations"; yet the rationale emerged with different—and wider—implications when the Ten Commandments were repeated in the book of Deuteronomy. There (Deuteronomy 5:11-14), the blessing of the day of rest included the whole household, even servants and animals; Shabbat was to serve as a reminder "that you were a servant in the land of Egypt, and the Lord your God brought you out thence by a mighty hand and an outstretched arm: therefore the Lord your God commanded you to keep Shabbat."

3   לַעֲשׂוֹת אֶת־הַשַּׁבָּת — OBSERVING THE SABBATH: The Hebrew verb is *la'asot*— literally, "to do, to make," and sometimes "to create." This reflects the idea that observance of Shabbat is a positive deed. Shabbat has been frequently thought of negatively, as a day on which many activities—held to constitute "work"—are forbidden. But the mood of Shabbat is one of active happiness and fulfillment. Far from being a dreary "thou shalt not," the key word is positive: *create* the Sabbath.

4   לְדֹרֹתָם — THROUGHOUT THEIR GENERATIONS: This foreshadows one of the most far-reaching passages in the Bible, in which Moses tells the assembled Israelites that the bond—"the covenant"—which has emerged between God and

בְּרִית עוֹלָם. |1
בֵּינִי וּבֵין בְּנֵי יִשְׂרָאֵל |2
אוֹת הִיא לְעֹלָם, |3

It is an everlasting covenant,
a sign between Me and the children
   of Israel forever.

berit olam. Beini uvein benei yisra'el ot hi le'olam,

Israel is to be a pattern of life for all time (Deuteronomy 5:3): "It was not with our fathers that God made this covenant, but with us, the living, every one of us who is here today." It is a thought which emerges with special appeal at the Passover Seder when we read—and accept—that each of us must feel as if he or she came out of Egypt. Jewish feeling and the Jewish role in the world seem, in this sense, to be timeless and unchanging.

בְּרִית עוֹלָם — AN EVERLASTING COVENANT: We read about the covenant with God all through the Bible. The Hebrew word *brit* brings to mind immediately the passage in the book of Genesis in which God puts before Abraham His promise of a glorious future for Abraham's descendants, and establishes circumcision as a sign of the covenant (*brit*) between God and the descendants of Abraham, throughout their generations (Genesis 17:10–13). A covenant involves mutual responsibilities. Repeatedly throughout the Bible, the terms are set: God will protect the people of Israel if they in turn fulfill His commandments—the moral law, and the rituals in which it is enshrined. |1

בֵּינִי וּבֵין בְּנֵי יִשְׂרָאֵל — BETWEEN ME AND THE CHILDREN OF ISRAEL: These words evoke the intimacy with God that has always existed in Jewish consciousness, as if the ancient Hebrews as a people were as close to God, in receiving the Ten Commandments, as Moses himself. There is a folktale that incorporates this motif of the people's direct contact with God, while at the same time recognizing the special role of Moses. The Talmud tells us that at the time of the revelation at Mount Sinai, at first the whole people heard the divine voice, but after they had heard the first two Commandments, they were so overcome with terror that they pleaded with Moses to be their sole representative, so that God could communicate the rest of the Commandments through him (Babylonian Talmud, *Makkot* 24a). |2

לְעוֹלָם — FOREVER: The striving to understand God's relationship with the universe and with mankind is renewed in every generation. From time immemorial, humanity has wrestled with the problem of understanding creation, both in scientific terms and with the poetry that imagination releases. The Rabbis, it is true, warned that speculation on these questions could be dangerous to peace of mind, or even to faith. Yet *ma'aseh bereshit* ("the act of creation") was an immensely fruitful subject for discussion among those held to be qualified. |3

כִּי־שֵׁשֶׁת יָמִים עָשָׂה יְיָ | 1

אֶת־הַשָּׁמַיִם וְאֶת־הָאָרֶץ,

וּבַיּוֹם הַשְּׁבִיעִי שָׁבַת וַיִּנָּפַשׁ. | 2,3,4

For in six days, the Lord made
Heaven and Earth,
and on the seventh day, He rested
and was refreshed.

ki sheshet yamim asah adonai et hashamayim ve'et ha'aretz,
uvayom hashevi'i shavat va-yinnafash.

---

1 עָשָׂה יְיָ אֶת־הַשָּׁמַיִם וְאֶת־הָאָרֶץ — THE LORD MADE HEAVEN AND EARTH: God as creator of the universe is projected majestically in this simple sentence. It echoes the poetic account of creation given in the opening chapters of the book of Genesis, even though the human mind could never fully understand what lies behind the cosmology that these words imply. In Jewish belief, the unified purpose of creation matches the unity of God who brought the universe into being, as expressed in the *Sh'ma.*

2 וּבַיּוֹם הַשְּׁבִיעִי — AND ON THE SEVENTH DAY: The number seven played an exceptionally important role in the lives of Semitic peoples and other peoples of antiquity. The seven-day week is, of course, approximately a quarter of the lunar month. In the Bible, seven is connected with many aspects of religious life (a more detailed discussion of this topic begins on p. 57).

3 שָׁבַת — HE RESTED: This one word *shavat* is enough to highlight the differences between the biblical creation story and other accounts of creation found among peoples in the ancient Near-Eastern world. The most important ancient parallel to the account in the book of Genesis is found in the Babylonian epic *Enuma Elish.* Here, as in Genesis, primeval chaos is a watery abyss which is separated into heaven and earth by a firmament. Day and night are created, followed by the luminaries. Man is the final act of creation, after which there is divine rest. But there are fundamental differences. In *Enuma Elish,* the watery chaos—*tehom* in Hebrew—is presented as an actual goddess, Tiamat; pagans saw creation as a primordial struggle between gods out of which a victorious god emerged. The Bible, however, demythologized the primitive pagan stories. Among the Hebrews, God is preexistent and omnipotent. The elements in nature are not mythologized as deities, but are part of the manifold works of God. Man is not an afterthought, but the pinnacle of creation. Above all, God is conceived of as bringing the universe into being for moral purpose. When God completes this supreme act of creation, and "sees" that it is good, and "rests," it is a holy moment that He extends to His people "throughout their generations."

4 וַיִּנָּפַשׁ — AND WAS REFRESHED: The Hebrew verb is formed from the noun *nefesh* ("soul"). *Va-yinnafash* is an echo of the account of the creation of man (Genesis 2:7): "And the Lord God formed man of the dust of the ground, and breathed into his nostrils the breath of life; and man became *nefesh ḥayyah*—a living soul."

Kaddish as a mourner's prayer is recited later
(p. 79). This shorter *Kaddish* (*Ḥatzi Kaddish*) marks
off different parts of the service.

ḤATZI KADDISH

חֲצִי קַדִּיש

1 יִתְגַּדַּל וְיִתְקַדַּשׁ שְׁמֵהּ רַבָּא
בְּעָלְמָא דִי בְרָא כִרְעוּתֵהּ.
וְיַמְלִיךְ מַלְכוּתֵהּ
בְּחַיֵּיכוֹן וּבְיוֹמֵיכוֹן
וּבְחַיֵּי דְכָל־בֵּית יִשְׂרָאֵל,
בַּעֲגָלָא וּבִזְמַן קָרִיב,
וְאִמְרוּ אָמֵן.

יְהֵא שְׁמֵהּ רַבָּא מְבָרַךְ,
לְעָלַם וּלְעָלְמֵי עָלְמַיָּא.

יִתְבָּרַךְ וְיִשְׁתַּבַּח וְיִתְפָּאַר,
וְיִתְרֹמַם וְיִתְנַשֵּׂא, וְיִתְהַדָּר
וְיִתְעַלֶּה וְיִתְהַלָּל שְׁמֵהּ דְּקֻדְשָׁא,
בְּרִיךְ הוּא,
לְעֵלָּא מִן כָּל־בִּרְכָתָא וְשִׁירָתָא
תֻּשְׁבְּחָתָא וְנֶחֱמָתָא
דַּאֲמִירָן בְּעָלְמָא,
וְאִמְרוּ אָמֵן.

Extolled and sanctified be the great
  name of God
In the world He created by His will.
May He establish His kingdom
  during your life, and during
  your days, and in the life of
  all the House of Israel, speedily
  and soon,
and say you: Amen.

May His great name be blessed
  forever and ever.
Blessed, praised, glorified, exalted,
  extolled and honored,
magnified and lauded be the name
  of the Holy One,
Blessed be He,
Though He be high above all
  blessings and hymns,
praises and consolations that are
  uttered in this world,
and say you: Amen.

Yehei shemei rabba mevarach, le'alam ul'almei almaya.

KADDISH: The word *kaddish* means "sanctification." This prayer, in its various forms, functions as a separator between different sections of the service. The short version found here is called the *Ḥatzi Kaddish* ("half *Kaddish*"). It serves in this case to prepare the congregation for the major prayer, the *Tefillah*, which is to follow. The *Kaddish Shalem* ("full *Kaddish*"; see p. 70) is usually recited by the *sheliaḥ tzibbur* ("conductor of the service") after the reading of the *Tefillah*. Two other versions, with slight variations, are the *Kaddish Derabbanan* ("scholars' *Kaddish*"), always recited after communal study in the synagogue, and the *Kaddish Yatom* ("mourners' *Kaddish*"; see p. 79), recited after the *Alenu* prayer. All forms of the *Kaddish* are in Aramaic, the spoken language of the Jews in late Temple times.

שְׁמֵהּ רַבָּא — THE GREAT NAME OF GOD: In Hebrew, these two Aramaic words—*shemeih rabba*—would be *shemo hagadol*. These words appear in the communal response, to which great importance is attached in the tradition.

1

The *Tefillah* ("prayer"), central to every
service, is a carefully designed structure of
prayers. It is also called the *Amidah*—
"the standing prayer"—because the
worshipers stand while reciting it.

TEFILLAH

תְּפִלָּה

אֲדֹנָי שְׂפָתַי תִּפְתָּח, וּפִי יַגִּיד תְּהִלָּתֶךָ.	1	Lord, open my lips that my mouth may declare Your praise.

RECITAL OF THE TEFILLAH: The *Tefillah* is recited in a very distinctive way, to signal its importance within the overall worship experience. As its alternate name *Amidah* indicates, it is recited standing, and, by old tradition "facing Jerusalem." It is a very personal act of worship, recited silently and without interruption.

FORMS OF THE TEFILLAH: On weekdays, when the *Tefillah* is recited at the morning, afternoon, and evening services, it is known as *tefillat shemoneh esrei* ("the *tefillah* of eighteen") because it originally consisted of eighteen blessings, subsequently increased to nineteen. On Shabbat and festivals, there are seven blessings (*tefillat sheva*); on Rosh Hashanah (New Year), there are nine (*tefillat tesha*).

STRUCTURE OF THE TEFILLAH: In all forms of the *Tefillah,* there are the same six basic blessings—three at the beginning and three at the end. On weekdays, there are, in addition, thirteen blessings, or petitions, framed by the six. In contrast, the *Tefillah* for Shabbat and festivals contains no similar series of petitions. On these occasions there is, in addition to the basic six blessings, a single central blessing, related to the special character of the day, called *kedushat ha-yom*— "sanctification of the day."

THE TEFILLAH ON SHABBAT: In the evening service as Shabbat begins, the central blessing is constructed around the passage which tells us that God rested on the seventh day, after creation (Genesis 2:1-3). In the morning service on Shabbat, the central blessing is linked to God's giving of the Ten Commandments at Mount Sinai. In the afternoon service, the emphasis is on Shabbat as a day of rest, a foretaste of the perfect peace which will characterize the messianic age. These three aspects of Shabbat—creation, revelation, redemption—are the three-tiered structure of Shabbat *Tefillah*.

SHABBAT AND WEEKDAY: The relative shortness of the Shabbat *Tefillah* expresses the difference that the rabbis saw *bein kodesh leḥol*—"between holiness and ordinary life." The series of petitions in the weekday *Tefillah* are heavily concerned with practicalities. Some deal with general human needs or longings; others with national aspirations, pleading for the end of "the dominion of arrogance" (the Roman domination) and the restoration of political freedom ("sound the great horn for our freedom . . . and gather us from the four corners of the earth"). Shabbat is kept free of these workaday worries. One surrenders in the *Tefillah* to deep issues of life and death, to restore one's peace of mind.

1   אֲדֹנָי שְׂפָתַי תִּפְתָּח — LORD, OPEN MY LIPS: This verse from the psalms (Psalm 51:17) is recited silently, to instill the mood of the *Tefillah*. After the *Tefillah*, another verse (Psalm 19:15) is recited in the same way.

The first blessing of the *Tefillah* anchors
the faith of the Jews in the historic experience of
the patriarchs—Abraham, Isaac, and Jacob.

AVOT

אָבוֹת

בָּרוּךְ אַתָּה יְיָ אֱלֹהֵינוּ וֵאלֹהֵי אֲבוֹתֵינוּ,	1,2	Be blessed, O Lord, our God and the God of our Fathers.

אֱלֹהֵינוּ — OUR GOD: Does our conception of God means the same to us as it did [1]
to our far-off ancestors? It is not easy to transpose ourselves to their time, but it is
certainly true that our memory of the patriarchs is a rock of our faith, for our bond
with these men is magically intimate. The world they lived in is totally remote; the
actuality of their lives is full of gaps; the moments of drama are episodic and
mysterious. Yet they are completely real to us. We are at home with them, we
share their fears and triumphs. Above all, we understand the power of their vision
when they developed the concept of one God, the Ruler of the universe. This
vision of the patriarchs became the pivot of faith for their descendants.

וֵאלֹהֵי אֲבוֹתֵינוּ — AND GOD OF OUR FATHERS: When we read the Bible and we [2]
encounter the Patriarchs praying to God; they seem to be dependent on Him in the
same way as later generations of Jews have been. Some scholars have offered a
different picture of patriarchal faith. They see the patriarchs as more limited in
their vision of a universal God. To these scholars, the patriarchal God was the god
of the clan, with each clan-leader claiming special protection for himself through
his own personal name for God. This, they argue, explains the different titles of
God in Genesis: "God of Abraham," "Revered One (*paḥad*) of Isaac," "Champion
(*avir*) of Jacob." But these titles, surviving from primitive times, are never incom-
patible with the biblical account, which rings true at every point, of Abraham
breaking away from his pagan Mesopotamian background to form a new concept
of God.

Abraham is a vivid figure in the biblical story, both as a benign head of his clan and
as the man who gave humanity, for the first time, a sense of the God who
fashioned and guides the universe. Not only Jews but followers of Christianity and
Islam as well look back in the same way to these images of Abraham.

Given the strength and warmth of this feeling, it is strange that some scholars
early in this century—following a lead from Bible scholarship in Germany—felt
called on to question whether the patriarchs had really existed! They pointed out,
correctly, that the patriarchs are not identified by name in any of the vast archaeo-
logical material covering their presumed existence—somewhere between 2000 and
1700 B.C.E.; the scholars argued that the stories about the patriarchs were made up
a thousand years later (or more) by historians and priests in order to show the
ancient origin of the Jewish belief in God.

Today, Bible scholars no longer go out of their way to break the mold of tradition
in this way. If the patriarchs themselves are not identified by archaeology, their

אֱלֹהֵי אַבְרָהָם אֱלֹהֵי יִצְחָק וֵאלֹהֵי יַעֲקֹב, הָאֵל הַגָּדֹל הַגִּבֹּר וְהַנּוֹרָא אֵל עֶלְיוֹן,	1 2	The God of Abraham, the God of Isaac and the God of Jacob. Great, mighty and awesome God, God on high,

setting is, and the details of that setting parallel the social, legal, economic and personal picture of that period now offered by scholarship. If the background was conveyed over a period of a few thousand years with such accuracy, "it is captious," says the scholar John Bright, "to deny that the leaders of the Hebrew clans did not bear the names that tradition retained for them."

1   אֱלֹהֵי יִצְחָק — THE GOD OF ISAAC: This identification is not an echo of the idea of some scholars, mentioned above, that each clan-leader built up his personal God. The fact that Jacob refers separately (Genesis 31:42, and elsewhere) to "the God of Abraham" (his grandfather) and *paḥad yitzḥak* ("the Revered One of Isaac," his father) merely builds up the continuity in allegiance to the same clan-god, strengthened further by the naming of *his* God—*avir ya'akov*, "the Champion of Jacob" (Genesis 49:24). The continuity of faith is established more clearly by the profusion of personal names among the ancient Hebrews which incorporate the word *el* ("God") or some Godlike attribute like *av* ("father") or *aḥ* ("brother") to yield: *Eliav* ("my God is a father to me"), *Avimelech* ("my divine Father is my King"), *Aḥiram* ("my divine Brother is exalted"). As John Bright says: "Such names illustrate splendidly the ancient nomad's keen sense of kinship between clan and deity: the God was the unseen head of the house; its members, the members of his family."

2   וֵאלֹהֵי יַעֲקֹב — AND THE GOD OF JACOB: Even if no one can replace "father Abraham" in our history and faith, we know his grandson Jacob more intimately, and in some respects more significantly. The Bible story of his adventures—his rivalry with his twin brother Esau, his flight to his cousins in Syria, his wives and concubines, his twelve sons, and, ultimately, the story of his favorite son Joseph— constitute an absorbing epic. It is in the earthy stories of Jacob's large family that we see the tiny clan of our ancestors turning into a people. Most significant for all future generations, including our own, is the mysterious episode in which Jacob wrestles with "a man" throughout the night. In the morning Jacob is told that henceforth he is to be called not Jacob but Israel, "for you wrestled (*sarita*) with God (*el*) and man, and prevailed" (Genesis 32:24–32). The name Jacob did in fact survive at the personal level, but from then on we became "the children of Israel" as a people.

גּוֹמֵל חֲסָדִים טוֹבִים | 1
וְקוֹנֵה הַכֹּל,
וְזוֹכֵר חַסְדֵי אָבוֹת,
וּמֵבִיא גוֹאֵל לִבְנֵי בְנֵיהֶם | 2
לְמַעַן שְׁמוֹ בְּאַהֲבָה.
מֶלֶךְ עוֹזֵר וּמוֹשִׁיעַ וּמָגֵן. | 3,4
בָּרוּךְ אַתָּה יְיָ, מָגֵן אַבְרָהָם. | 5

God, whose acts bestow grace and who embraces all.
He remembers the grace of the Fathers,
And will bring a redeemer to their children's children,
Fulfilling His name, in love.
O King, helper, savior and shield.
Be blessed, O Lord, shield of Abraham.

גּוֹמֵל חֲסָדִים טוֹבִים — WHOSE ACTS BESTOW GRACE: *Ḥesed* is often translated **1** "lovingkindness." The word *ḥasid*, "a pious man," is from this root. In turning to the God of Abraham, Isaac, and Jacob, we hear in this prayer the echo between God's many acts of grace and the grace of the patriarchs.

גּוֹאֵל — A REDEEMER: To those who composed this prayer, the word *go'el* **2** ("redeemer") did not suggest a supernatural being who would come to earth to save mankind. Rather, it brings to mind God's innumerable acts of redemption, starting with His deliverance of the Israelites from bondage in Egypt.

מֶלֶךְ — KING: The concept of God as King goes back to the most primitive times, **3** so that we accept it easily in a prayer that harks back to the archaic days of the patriarchs. In the pagan world of the second millenium B.C.E., when the patriarchs lived, the Canaanite gods were thought of as a kind of royal house, with *El Elyon*, the chief god, as king. But the Hebrews, as far back as Abraham, were never confused by the pagan conception. The Hebrews thought of God as King, as the only God, the unique, independent and all-powerful Creator and Ruler of the universe. The distinction from their pagan neighbors survived when the Hebrews established their monarchy. The kings whom they chose had regal authority, but never the divine status attributed to kings of other nations. God the King was never to be compared with human monarchs.

עוֹזֵר — HELPER: Through our feeling for the patriarchs, we acknowledge our **4** fallibility, for as human beings, the patriarchs were as limited and fallible as we are ourselves. This, indeed, is central to the hold that they have on our affections. In the stories built up around them, we see them struggling with the workaday problems of earning a living, keeping peace with their neighbors, and trying to soften, as best they can, their own family jealousies and quarrels. God is not just our "King"; He helps us in times of personal trouble.

מָגֵן אַבְרָהָם — SHIELD OF ABRAHAM: These words echo a famous passage in **5** which the word of God came to Abraham in a vision: "Fear not, Abram: I am a shield to you" (Genesis 15:1).

In this second blessing of the *Tefillah,* we
turn to God as the sustainer of life.

GEVUROT

גְּבוּרוֹת

אַתָּה גִבּוֹר לְעוֹלָם יְיָ,	1	You are the eternal Power, O Lord, renewing life beyond death— mighty in salvation.
מְחַיֵּה מֵתִים אַתָּה,	2	
רַב לְהוֹשִׁיעַ.		
In winter seasons, we add:		In winter seasons, we add:
מַשִּׁיב הָרוּחַ וּמוֹרִיד הַגֶּשֶׁם.	3	He causes the wind to blow and the rain to fall.
מְכַלְכֵּל חַיִּים בְּחֶסֶד,	4	You sustain life with loving- kindness; You renew life beyond death with unending mercy.
מְחַיֵּה מֵתִים בְּרַחֲמִים רַבִּים.		

1   גִבּוֹר — POWER: The Hebrew word *gibor* gives the name to this section of the *Tefillah: gevurot.* The essence of God's power is that he gives life to humanity. This idea is projected, as we shall see, into the belief that the human spirit does not disappear with death.

2   מְחַיֵּה מֵתִים — RENEWING LIFE BEYOND DEATH: Literally, these words mean: "who brings the dead to life." A belief in physical resurrection was widespread among Jews. The way this idea was understood is discussed in detail at the conclusion of this blessing, which concludes with these same words (p. 55). In the rest of this blessing, God's beneficent power is extolled in terms easier for humanity to grasp.

3   וּמוֹרִיד הַגֶּשֶׁם — HE CAUSES . . . THE RAIN TO FALL: In ancient days in the Holy Land, our ancestors were sharply aware of the utter dependence of humanity on the regular ordering of nature. The miracle of the seasons was central—the drought of a burning summer yielded to the fresh start of life in the "New Year" (*Rosh Hashanah*) of autumn, the harshness of winter vanished before the fertility of spring. Jews expressed appreciation for this on the festivals with special prayers for rain and harvests; but here in the *Tefillah* God's power is celebrated in broad poetic terms. God sustains us in life—"healing the sick, releasing the captive"—with the same lovingkindness that sustains nature itself.

4   מְכַלְכֵּל חַיִּים — YOU SUSTAIN LIFE: This is a perpetual theme in the psalms—the power of God to help those afflicted with enmity and distress: "You support those who fall, heal the sick. . . ." The psalmist wrote: "The Lord is my strength and my shield; my heart trusts in Him. I was helped, and my heart exulted. I will glorify Him with my song" (Psalm 28:7).

סוֹמֵךְ נוֹפְלִים, וְרוֹפֵא חוֹלִים,		You support those who fall, heal the sick, release the captives,
וּמַתִּיר אֲסוּרִים,	1	
וּמְקַיֵּם אֱמוּנָתוֹ לִישֵׁנֵי עָפָר.		and keep faith with those that sleep in the dust.
מִי כָמוֹךָ בַּעַל גְּבוּרוֹת	2,3	Who is like unto You, Lord of Power?
וּמִי דּוֹמֶה לָּךְ,		Who is compared to You, O King, in whose hands are death and life, and who causes salvation to spring forth?
מֶלֶךְ מֵמִית וּמְחַיֶּה		
וּמַצְמִיחַ יְשׁוּעָה.	4	

וּמַתִּיר אֲסוּרִים — RELEASE THE CAPTIVES: A Jew released after being held as a hostage or for ransom or for other reasons would thank God in a brief public ceremony in the synagogue after the reading of the Torah; but he would be aware, too, of how much his fellow Jews had helped at the practical level. In nothing was Jewish kinship expressed more strongly than in the priority given to this *mitzvah* ("religious obligation") of ransoming a captive. Levies were made on Jewish communities everywhere to establish funds for this purpose; rules were laid down in the Talmud, and in later works, to secure releases with speed and efficiency. For the dangers of our own time, the story of Rabbi Meir of Rothenburg, who lived in the thirteenth century, is vividly appropriate. When he was thrown into prison, he issued an order forbidding Jews to ransom him, in order to avoid setting a precedent which would encourage despots to take rabbis as hostages so as to secure high ransoms. 1

מִי כָמוֹךָ — WHO IS LIKE UNTO YOU? This is one of the many echoes in the prayerbook of the shout of triumph from the Song of Moses (Exodus 15:11). 2

בַּעַל גְּבוּרוֹת — LORD OF POWER: This Hebrew phrase, *ba'al gevurot*, echoes the theme of this section—*gevurot*. 3

וּמַצְמִיחַ יְשׁוּעָה — WHO CAUSES SALVATION TO SPRING FORTH: In the eyes of the sages, "salvation" (*yeshu'ah*) is not a state of individual perfection achieved by faith. It is a regeneration of society in which the moral life, as preached by the prophets, would "spring forth" everywhere: "The Lord shall be King over all the earth; on that day there shall be one God, and His name One" (Zechariah 14:9). This ideal is universal in its scope; the prophets believed that Jews exist in the world as a step towards this ideal, so that their preservation as a religious people is an essential prerequisite for the "salvation" that God will bring to the world. 4

וְנֶאֱמָן אַתָּה לְהַחֲיוֹת מֵתִים. בָּרוּךְ אַתָּה יְיָ, מְחַיֵּה הַמֵּתִים.	1	Our faith is in You to renew life beyond death Be blessed, O Lord, who renews life beyond death.

1   מְחַיֵּה מֵתִים — LIFE BEYOND DEATH: Each of us reads a personal meaning into the concept of immortality. As noted above, Jews believed for centuries—and many still do—in *physical* resurrection, interpreting literally the words of this blessing: *meḥayyeh ha-metim*—"He brings the dead to life." The Pharisees, prominent in the last century B.C.E., were the first Jews to express a belief in immortality, in contrast to the Sadducees, who held that as the doctrine was not mentioned in the Bible, it had no validity. The sages were never specific in philosophic terms about the nature of immortality, though they were sure that Jews—and righteous non-Jews—could count on a place in "the world to come." More fancifully, they felt free to indulge in ideas about the blissful conditions of Paradise.

The idea of physical resurrection gathered strength among Jews during the Middle Ages, the concept being that after the Messiah had come, Jews would "roll underground" from the four corners of the Diaspora to rise in the Holy Land. (For this reason, many pious Jews sought burial in the Holy Land, with the implication that they would be at rest, ready for the new life.)

Although even rationalist philosophers held that belief in immortality was a cardinal doctrine of Judaism, they deemphasized the physical aspect and concentrated on the immortality of the soul. Drawing on the belief that God created humanity with a purpose, they felt—as many still feel—that the soul survives; it is inconceivable that mankind, given life by God for a reason, should disappear into emptiness.

The mystery is impenetrable, yet faith demands some words to express it in human terms. Some have replaced "He brings the dead to life" by *meḥayyeh ha-kol*—"He gives life to all"; but the traditional words linger in the mind more acceptably, even if one has to call on parable and poetry to understand them.

Parable is often alive and stimulating where reason can be uninspiring. One parable illustrates what a pious *ḥasid* called Moses thought about life and death. He dreamed that he was in paradise and was conducted to a room in which the *Tanna'im*—founding fathers of the Talmud—were studying the Torah. "Is this all there is to paradise?" he asked. A voice was heard: "Moses, you believe that the *Tanna'im* are in paradise. You are wrong. Paradise is in the *Tanna'im*."

This is the third basic blessing
of the *Tefillah,* with repeated emphasis
on the word *kadosh*—"holy."

KEDUSHAT HASHEM

קְדֻשַּׁת הַשֵּׁם

אַתָּה קָדוֹשׁ וְשִׁמְךָ קָדוֹשׁ,	1	You are holy, Your name is holy,
וּקְדוֹשִׁים בְּכָל־יוֹם	2	and the holy ones praise You daily.
יְהַלְלוּךָ סֶּלָה.	3	*Selah!*
בָּרוּךְ אַתָּה יְיָ, הָאֵל הַקָּדוֹשׁ.	4	Be blessed, O Lord, the holy God.

אַתָּה קָדוֹשׁ — YOU ARE HOLY: This third blessing of the *Tefillah* is known as **1**
Kedushat Hashem—"the sanctification of The Name," meaning the sanctification of
God. Here, the *Tefillah* moves into the mysterious realm of holiness. To say that
God is "holy" (*kadosh*) expresses something indefinable, compounded of the venera-
tion and awe in which we hold Him. The great German theologian Rudolph Otto
called the idea of the holy "the mysterium tremendum." God is the fount of
holiness; through our relationships with Him, we seek to bring the feeling of
sanctity and dedication into our own lives.

וּקְדוֹשִׁים — THE HOLY ONES: In the spirit of this blessing, this word seems to **2**
evoke Isaiah's vision in which he sees the angelic seraphim—each with six wings—
surrounding God on His throne, and calling one to the other: "Holy, holy, holy is
the Lord of hosts; the whole earth is full of His glory" (Isaiah 6:2-3).

סֶּלָה — SELAH: No one is sure of the etymology or meaning of this term, which **3**
appears frequently in the psalms, usually at the end of a verse or at the end of the
whole psalm. Some have taken it to be a musical notation; others see it as a kind of
affirmation—like Amen—of the sense of the verse. It seems to be used as an
affirmation in the present blessing, where the word *yehallelucha* ("praise You")
brings to mind the *hallel* ("praise") of the psalms.

הָאֵל הַקָּדוֹשׁ — THE HOLY GOD: The expression of God's holiness in this bless- **4**
ing is reinforced when the *Tefillah* is repeated in some services by the cantor, with
responses by the congregation. At those services, if a *minyan* ("quorum") of ten is
present, a special liturgical expression of praise is inserted here, drawing from
Isaiah's vision of God on His throne surrounded by seraphim (Isaiah 6:2-3). The
cantor calls on the congregation to sanctify God's name "as they sanctify it in the
highest heavens," where the seraphim cry "Holy, holy, holy is the Lord of hosts;
the whole earth is full of His glory." (A more accurate and revealing translation is:
"the fullness of the whole earth is His glory.") The second response of the congregation is: "Blessed be the glory of the Lord from His place" (Ezekiel 3:12). The third
response is a verse from the psalms: "The Lord shall reign forever and ever; thy
God, O Zion, unto all generations" (Psalm 146:10).

This central blessing of the *Tefillah*
concentrates on the holiness of Shabbat (Kedushat Hayom).
It is inserted between the opening three and the
closing three basic blessings of the *Tefillah*.

KEDUSHAT HAYOM

קְדֻשַּׁת הַיּוֹם

אַתָּה קִדַּשְׁתָּ אֶת־יוֹם הַשְּׁבִיעִי לִשְׁמֶךָ, תַּכְלִית מַעֲשֵׂה שָׁמַיִם וָאָרֶץ. וּבֵרַכְתּוֹ מִכָּל־הַיָּמִים, וְקִדַּשְׁתּוֹ מִכָּל־הַזְּמַנִּים, וְכֵן כָּתוּב בְּתוֹרָתֶךָ:	1,2	You have sanctified the seventh day to Your name— The completion of the creation of heaven and earth. You have blessed it above other days, and sanctified it above other seasons, and thus is it written in Your Torah:

1 אַתָּה קִדַּשְׁתָּ — YOU HAVE SANCTIFIED: This is spelled out in the passage from the book of Genesis included later in this prayer: "God blessed the seventh day and sanctified it." The sanctity of the day of rest is a wholly original religious idea. It has permeated Jewish life since biblical times, after it was first dramatically expressed as one of the Ten Commandments.

There are two somewhat differing versions of the Ten Commandments in the Bible. In the first, in the book of Exodus, Shabbat is linked explicitly to God's rest on the seventh day of creation: "wherefore God blessed the Sabbath day and sanctified it" (Exodus 20:8-11). In the Deuteronomy version, creation is not mentioned but only implied. The seventh day is stated to be "the Sabbath of the Lord your God" (Deuteronomy 5:12-15); identifying with this, a Jew has to ensure the same kind of "holy rest" for the entire household, including servants, visitors and animals. The rest given to servants is to remind Jews of the miracle of their deliverance from being slaves themselves in Egypt: "therefore the Lord your God commanded you to keep the Sabbath day." The holiness of Shabbat thus receives two forms of expression, and its overpowering significance dwarfs the differences in rationale. In the book of Exodus, as one scholar puts it, "the rationale is cosmic-sacramental"; in the book of Deuteronomy, it is "historical-humanistic."

2 יוֹם הַשְּׁבִיעִי — THE SEVENTH DAY: This phrase too comes from the account of creation from the book of Genesis, which appears as the next paragraph of the *Tefillah*. As noted briefly earlier, the number seven was important to all peoples of the ancient world. Scholars tell us that it was sacred not only to Semitic peoples, but also to Egyptians, Persians, and the Vedic folk of India. Some link it to the realization that the seven-day week is an almost exact division of the lunar month of twenty-nine days. Others argue that the importance of seven in the pagan world was derived from the worship of the seven heavenly bodies—the sun, the moon, and the five planets. From whatever origin, the number seven is significant

Genesis 2:1-3

וַיְכֻלּוּ הַשָּׁמַיִם וְהָאָרֶץ
וְכָל־צְבָאָם.
וַיְכַל אֱלֹהִים בַּיּוֹם הַשְּׁבִיעִי
מְלַאכְתּוֹ אֲשֶׁר עָשָׂה,
וַיִּשְׁבֹּת בַּיּוֹם הַשְּׁבִיעִי
מִכָּל־מְלַאכְתּוֹ אֲשֶׁר עָשָׂה.
וַיְבָרֶךְ אֱלֹהִים אֶת־יוֹם הַשְּׁבִיעִי
וַיְקַדֵּשׁ אֹתוֹ,
כִּי בוֹ שָׁבַת מִכָּל־מְלַאכְתּוֹ
אֲשֶׁר בָּרָא אֱלֹהִים לַעֲשׂוֹת.

1

"Heaven and earth were complete,
   with all their array.
On the seventh day God completed
   the work He had done.
He rested on the seventh day from
   all the work He had done.
And God blessed the seventh day
   and sanctified it,
for on this day God ceased from all
   the work of Creation that He
   had done."

---

repeatedly in the Bible. In the story of the Flood, Noah is to take clean animals and "the birds of the air" into the Ark "by sevens." The Flood itself was to begin in seven days. Numerous rituals later revolved around seven: sacramental purity often involved isolation for seven days; the eating of *matzah* on Passover, according to the biblical account, is for seven days; the consecration of the priests was to take seven days. The *menorah* of the Tabernacle in the desert (and later the *menorah* of the Holy Temple) was to have seven lights, three on either side and one in the middle. When Joshua marched on Jericho, seven priests blowing on seven trumpets compassed the city seven times before the walls fell. These are just a few examples of how seven, and multiples of seven, are significant in the Bible. Other examples include the sabbatical year (the land was to lie fallow every seventh year) and the jubilee year (after a cycle of seven sabbatical years).

וַיְבָרֶךְ אֱלֹהִים אֶת־יוֹם הַשְּׁבִיעִי — AND GOD BLESSED THE SEVENTH DAY: From the beginning, the ancient Hebrews saw something sacred in the concept of Shabbat, and looked for ways to link this to the holiness they saw in God. As long ago as the eighth century B.C.E., the prophet Hosea warned that it would be a sign of God's anger if He would "cause all Israel's mirth to cease, her feast days, her new moons and her Sabbaths" (Hosea 2:13).

Scholars tell us that the tradition of Shabbat observance grew stronger during the Babylonian Exile (sixth century B.C.E.) and after the return from Babylonia (fifth century B.C.E.). During the period of the Exile, religious leaders had to fight against assimilation; Shabbat tradition was strongly emphasized as a way of distinguishing Jews from those around them. Ezekiel, a prophet of the Exile, speaks of God making Shabbat the crucial element in Israel's existence: "I gave them My Sabbaths, to be a sign between Me and them, that they might know that I am the Lord who sanctifies them" (Ezekiel 20:12).

1

אֱלֹהֵינוּ וֵאלֹהֵי אֲבוֹתֵינוּ,	Our God, God of our Fathers, may our rest be pleasing to You.
רְצֵה בִמְנוּחָתֵנוּ.	
קַדְּשֵׁנוּ בְּמִצְוֹתֶיךָ,	Sanctify us with Your *mitzvot*, let the Torah be our way of life.
וְתֵן חֶלְקֵנוּ בְּתוֹרָתֶךָ.	
שַׂבְּעֵנוּ מִטּוּבֶךָ,	Satisfy us with Your goodness, gladden us with Your salvation.
וְשַׂמְּחֵנוּ בִּישׁוּעָתֶךָ,	
וְטַהֵר לִבֵּנוּ לְעָבְדְּךָ בֶּאֱמֶת.	Purify our hearts to serve You truthfully.
וְהַנְחִילֵנוּ יְיָ אֱלֹהֵינוּ	Let Your holy Sabbath be our heritage, O Lord our God,
בְּאַהֲבָה וּבְרָצוֹן שַׁבַּת קָדְשֶׁךָ,	In love and favor;
וְיָנוּחוּ בָהּ יִשְׂרָאֵל מְקַדְּשֵׁי שְׁמֶךָ.	May all Israel, who sanctify Your name, find rest in it.
בָּרוּךְ אַתָּה יְיָ, מְקַדֵּשׁ הַשַּׁבָּת.	Be blessed, O Lord, who sanctifies the Sabbath.

The numbers 1, 2, 3 appear alongside the Hebrew and English text.

---

1 רְצֵה בִמְנוּחָתֵנוּ — MAY OUR REST BE PLEASING TO YOU: The idea of "pleasing" God lies deep in the Jewish faith. In human terms, we are happy to please someone we love or respect. How do we conceive of God, who created the universe, taking pleasure from the way we observe Shabbat?

In the Bible, the concept is used particularly to indicate God's "pleasure" at sacrifices offered to Him in the Temple. There was no reward or absolution through a sacrifice itself; it was the Temple visit that made the worshiper ask—as the synagogue visit does today—whether he or she is leading the kind of life that will "please" God. The prophet Amos expressed this in one of the most famous passages in the Bible. God "is not pleased" (*lo ertzeh*) with sacrifices, unless "justice wells up like water, and righteousness like a mighty stream" (Amos 5:24).

2 מִטּוּבֶךָ — WITH YOUR GOODNESS: How does one ascribe a human quality like "goodness" to God, whose uniqueness seems to bar ordinary description? Jewish theologians, considering this question, drew a distinction between "essential attributes" of God, and "attributes of action." The essential attributes, centering on God's existence, are indefinable.

3 וְיָנוּחוּ בָהּ — FIND REST IN IT: The Shabbat *menuḥah* ("rest") has been a unique bounty to Jews throughout their history. The word conveys a mixture of holiness and human satisfaction. This is the true miracle of Shabbat.

This blessing, the first of the last three
of the *Tefillah*, speaks nostalgically of worship
(*avodah*) in the Temple of Jerusalem.

AVODAH

עֲבוֹדָה

רְצֵה יְיָ אֱלֹהֵינוּ בְּעַמְּךָ יִשְׂרָאֵל וּבִתְפִלָּתָם,	1	Be pleased, O Lord our God, with Your people Israel and their prayer;
וְהָשֵׁב אֶת הָעֲבוֹדָה לִדְבִיר בֵּיתֶךָ.	2	Restore our worship to the oracle of Your house.
וְאִשֵּׁי יִשְׂרָאֵל וּתְפִלָּתָם בְּאַהֲבָה תְקַבֵּל בְּרָצוֹן,		Receive in love and pleasure the sacrifices of Israel and their prayer.
וּתְהִי לְרָצוֹן תָּמִיד עֲבֹדַת יִשְׂרָאֵל עַמֶּךָ.		May the service of Your people Israel be pleasing to You forever.

On Rosh Ḥodesh, we say:

אֱלֹהֵינוּ וֵאלֹהֵי אֲבוֹתֵינוּ,		Our God and God of our Fathers:
יַעֲלֶה וְיָבֹא וְיַגִּיעַ,	3	May there rise before You— May it come and reach and be seen and be pleasing and be heard and be noted and remembered—
וְיֵרָאֶה וְיֵרָצֶה וְיִשָּׁמַע,		
וְיִפָּקֵד וְיִזָּכֵר זִכְרוֹנֵנוּ וּפִקְדוֹנֵנוּ,		Our memory and history,
וְזִכְרוֹן אֲבוֹתֵינוּ וְזִכְרוֹן מָשִׁיחַ בֶּן דָּוִד עַבְדֶּךָ,		The memory of our Fathers, The memory of the Messiah, son of David Your servant,
וְזִכְרוֹן יְרוּשָׁלַיִם עִיר קָדְשֶׁךָ,		The memory of Jerusalem Your holy city,
וְזִכְרוֹן כָּל-עַמְּךָ בֵּית יִשְׂרָאֵל לְפָנֶיךָ,		The memory of all Your people, the House of Israel.

רְצֵה — BE PLEASED: The hope for God's "pleasure" (*retzeh*) is linked to the "pleasure" that God took from sacrifices at the Temple— if the worship was an expression of religious feeling and not an empty ritual. **1**

לִדְבִיר בֵּיתֶךָ — TO THE ORACLE OF YOUR HOUSE: This prayer was composed soon after the fall of the Temple by Jews longing for its restoration. Few of us today wish to see the sacrificial system restored, but in reading this prayer, we unite ourselves with the spirit of those who expressed for endless centuries their love of Jerusalem. **2**

יַעֲלֶה — MAY THERE RISE: This occasional prayer, with its use of almost repetitive synonyms—"rise," "come," "reach," etc.—catches the joyous spirit of a relatively minor festival in which one is nevertheless free to enjoy a splurge of excitement. After this florid opening, the prayer works around to specifying the occasion—Rosh Ḥodesh (new month) or the intermediate days of Pesaḥ (Passover) or Sukkot (Tabernacles); but throughout, the theme is the one already identified: the love of Zion and the prayer for its restoration. **3**

לִפְלֵיטָה לְטוֹבָה, לְחֵן וּלְחֶסֶד וּלְרַחֲמִים, לְחַיִּים וּלְשָׁלוֹם, בְּיוֹם רֹאשׁ הַחֹדֶשׁ הַזֶּה. זָכְרֵנוּ יְיָ אֱלֹהֵינוּ בּוֹ לְטוֹבָה, וּפָקְדֵנוּ בוֹ לִבְרָכָה, וְהוֹשִׁיעֵנוּ בוֹ לְחַיִּים.	**1** May it bring deliverance and well-being, grace, lovingkindness and mercy, life and peace on this Rosh Hodesh Day. Remember us, O Lord our God, for our well-being; be mindful of us for blessing; save us for life.
וּבִדְבַר יְשׁוּעָה וְרַחֲמִים חוּס וְחָנֵּנוּ, וְרַחֵם עָלֵינוּ וְהוֹשִׁיעֵנוּ, כִּי אֵלֶיךָ עֵינֵינוּ, כִּי אֵל מֶלֶךְ חַנּוּן וְרַחוּם אָתָּה.	**2** With Your promise of salvation and mercy, spare us and be gracious to us, have mercy on us and save us; we turn our eyes to You, for You are a gracious and merciful God and King.
וְתֶחֱזֶינָה עֵינֵינוּ בְּשׁוּבְךָ לְצִיּוֹן בְּרַחֲמִים. בָּרוּךְ אַתָּה יְיָ, הַמַּחֲזִיר שְׁכִינָתוֹ לְצִיּוֹן.	O let our eyes see Your return to Zion in mercy. Be blessed, O Lord, who will restore His presence to Zion. **3**

1   לִפְלֵיטָה — MAY IT BRING DELIVERANCE: Here, the Messianic Age is seen as a deliverance from "the oppressors"—the Romans and their successors. The Messiah, a descendant of King David, will arrive on earth to break the yoke of the heathen and to reign over a world of "well-being, grace, lovingkindness, mercy, life and peace."

2   וּבִדְבַר יְשׁוּעָה — WITH YOUR PROMISE OF SALVATION: Salvation (*yeshu'ah*) is treated here in general terms. In postbiblical times, when the concept of an idyllic age to come gained widespread acceptance, it was common, though not universal, for a personal Messiah to be included as the basis for that concept. Some sources (the Dead Sea Scrolls, for example) predicted that deliverance would come through *two* figures, a "priest of righteousness" (*kohen tzedek*) and a Davidic king.

There are many references in the literature of the Second Temple period to men who claimed to be the Messiah, notably in the writings of Josephus. Lineage from King David was always assumed; but though the claimant might have had some supernatural qualities, he was always human, and had to prove his status by his deeds of salvation.

3   הַמַּחֲזִיר שְׁכִינָתוֹ לְצִיּוֹן — WHO WILL RESTORE HIS PRESENCE TO ZION: The deeds of a messianic warrior, defeating oppression and ushering in a realm of moral perfection, are only an outward expression of the true meaning of a messianic age, symbolized supremely in the concept of God's "return" to Zion.

61

This blessing, the second-to-last of the
Tefillah, is a proud and public affirmation (*hodayah*) of faith.
The confidence of *Modim* lifts the heart,
like a change in music from minor to major.

HODAYAH

הוֹדָיָה

1 מוֹדִים אֲנַחְנוּ לָךְ שָׁאַתָּה הוּא
יְיָ אֱלֹהֵינוּ וֵאלֹהֵי אֲבוֹתֵינוּ
לְעוֹלָם וָעֶד.
צוּר חַיֵּינוּ מָגֵן יִשְׁעֵנוּ אַתָּה הוּא.
2 לְדוֹר וָדוֹר נוֹדֶה לָּךְ
וּנְסַפֵּר תְּהִלָּתֶךָ
עַל חַיֵּינוּ הַמְּסוּרִים בְּיָדֶךָ,
וְעַל נִשְׁמוֹתֵינוּ הַפְּקוּדוֹת לָךְ,
וְעַל נִסֶּיךָ שֶׁבְּכָל־יוֹם עִמָּנוּ,
וְעַל נִפְלְאוֹתֶיךָ וְטוֹבוֹתֶיךָ
3 שֶׁבְּכָל־עֵת, עֶרֶב וָבֹקֶר
וְצָהֳרָיִם,
4 הַטּוֹב כִּי לֹא כָלוּ רַחֲמֶיךָ,
וְהַמְרַחֵם כִּי לֹא תַמּוּ חֲסָדֶיךָ.
מֵעוֹלָם קִוִּינוּ לָךְ.
	We declare in thanksgiving that You
	   are our Lord God, and the God
	   of our Fathers, forever and ever.
	You are the rock of our lives,
	   the Shield of our salvation.
	Through all generations, we thank
	   You and declare Your praise,
	   for our lives which are in Your
	   hand, for our souls which are in
	   Your keeping,
	For the miracle of Your being which
	   is with us daily,
	For Your wonders and benefactions
	   at all times, at morning, noon,
	   and eventide,
	You are goodness itself: Your
	   mercies never cease;
	You are the merciful one, Your acts
	   of grace never end: Since time
	   began, we have put our hope in
	   You.

1 מוֹדִים אֲנַחְנוּ — WE DECLARE IN THANKSGIVING: The opening word *modim* (literally, "we thank") has a soft resonance in Hebrew, which makes this moment in the *Tefillah* very familiar to worshipers. Indeed, this blessing has been known as *Modim* since Temple times.

2 לְדוֹר וָדוֹר — THROUGH ALL GENERATIONS: History, to Jews, is the unwinding of a continuous story which has had a recognizable pattern in the unending dialogue that we have had with God. Two thousand years ago, our ancestors recited this blessing with the light of sacrificial fires filling the Temple, while Levites sang the Psalms of David to the accompaniment of trumpet and lyre. Today, in a very different world, *Modim* still speaks to us as a prayer of love.

3 עֶרֶב וָבֹקֶר וְצָהֳרָיִם — MORNING, NOON, AND EVENTIDE: The order of the words is more euphonious in English this way, though in Hebrew the words are "eve, morning, and noon," because the day begins, as with Shabbat, on the preceding evening.

4 הַטּוֹב — YOU ARE GOODNESS ITSELF: The literal translation is: "the good one." In a sequence of attributes, we move from goodness to mercies, and thence, naturally, to acts of grace.

וְעַל כֻּלָּם יִתְבָּרַךְ וְיִתְרוֹמַם שִׁמְךָ
מַלְכֵּנוּ תָּמִיד לְעוֹלָם וָעֶד.
1 וְכֹל הַחַיִּים יוֹדוּךָ סֶּלָה,
וִיהַלְלוּ אֶת־שִׁמְךָ בֶּאֱמֶת,
הָאֵל יְשׁוּעָתֵנוּ וְעֶזְרָתֵנוּ סֶלָה.
בָּרוּךְ אַתָּה יְיָ
הַטּוֹב שִׁמְךָ וּלְךָ נָאֶה לְהוֹדוֹת.

For all these things may Your name,
O our King, be blessed and
exalted forever and ever.
1 Let all the living give thanks to You.
Selah!
Let them praise Your name in truth,
O God, our salvation and our
support. *Selah!*
Be blessed, O Lord, whose name is
goodness itself, and to whom it
is meet to give thanks.

1 וְכֹל הַחַיִּים יוֹדוּךָ — LET ALL THE LIVING GIVE THANKS: This idea is exqui-
sitely expressed in a famous poem by Judah Halevi (1075–c. 1141), who adorned
the Golden Age of Moorish Spain. Judah Halevi was a philosopher as well as a
poet, and in this poem he welds the two realms of philosophy and poetry together.
At one level in the poem, the poet considers God a Being who can be near to him,
and speaks to him as if to a person; at another level, he sees God as the whole of
the living universe, too huge a concept for man to take in.

The opening lines are pantheistic:

Lord where shall I find You? Your place is lofty and secret.
And where shall I not find You? The whole earth is full of Your glory.

Then, the poet begins to explore the paradoxes of faith:

You are found in man's innermost heart, yet You fixed earth's boundaries.
You are a strong tower for those who are near, and the trust of those who are
far.
You are enthroned on the cherubim, above the Ark, yet You dwell in the
heights of heaven . . .
The sphere of heaven cannot contain You; how much less the chambers of the
Temple.

From the majesty of these words, the poet turns back to the simple faith of one
who knows God in his own life:

Who can say that he has not seen You? The heavens and their legions
proclaim Your dread—without a sound:
But can God really dwell among men? Their foundations are dust: what can
they conceive of Him?
O Holy One, make Your home where they sing Your praises and Your glory.
The living creatures, standing on the summit of the world, praise Your
wonders.
Your throne is above their heads, yet it is You who carries them all.

This is the last of the blessings of the *Tefillah*.
It evokes the moment in the Temple
service at which the priests recited their
special prayer for peace *(shalom)*.

SHALOM

שָׁלוֹם

1 שָׁלוֹם רָב עַל יִשְׂרָאֵל עַמְּךָ תָּשִׂים לְעוֹלָם, כִּי אַתָּה הוּא מֶלֶךְ אָדוֹן לְכָל־הַשָּׁלוֹם. 2 וְטוֹב בְּעֵינֶיךָ לְבָרֵךְ אֶת־עַמְּךָ יִשְׂרָאֵל בְּכָל־עֵת וּבְכָל־שָׁעָה בִּשְׁלוֹמֶךָ. 3 בָּרוּךְ אַתָּה יְיָ, הַמְבָרֵךְ אֶת־עַמּוֹ יִשְׂרָאֵל בַּשָּׁלוֹם.	Grant abundant peace to Your people Israel forever. You are the sovereign Lord of peace. May it be good in Your sight to bless Your people Israel at all times and in every hour with Your peace. Blessed be the Lord, who will bless His people Israel with peace.

שָׁלוֹם רָב — GRANT ABUNDANT PEACE: The priestly benediction—"May the Lord bless you and keep you" (Numbers 6:22-26)—ends with a prayer for peace. The priestly blessing was recited daily in the Temple, and this paragraph in the *Tefillah*—going back to the Talmud—is in place of this. **1**

וְטוֹב בְּעֵינֶיךָ — MAY IT BE GOOD IN YOUR SIGHT: The concept of God's peace as it is expressed in the priestly benediction (Numbers 6:22-26) is referred to in the prayerbook as "the threefold blessing." The first clause—"may the Lord keep you"—is held to refer to the physical peace which is secured through God's protection. The second clause—"may the Lord's face . . . shine upon you"—refers to the inward spiritual peace that man seeks through turning to God. The third clause—"may the Lord lift up his face to you"—is the peace which flows from God to man when harmony is achieved. This last blessing of the *Tefillah* therefore brings together all that has been felt in the service so far, and prepares us for the moment when we will carry these feelings with us into the world outside. **2**

הַמְבָרֵךְ אֶת־עַמּוֹ יִשְׂרָאֵל בַּשָּׁלוֹם — WHO WILL BLESS HIS PEOPLE ISRAEL WITH PEACE: The Christian theologian Emil Kautzsch wrote of the priestly blessing: "In beautiful climax, it leads in three clauses from the petition for material blessing and protection to that for the favor of God as spiritual blessing, and finally to the bestowal of the *shalom*, the peace or welfare in which all material and spiritual well-being is comprehended." This echoes the words of the great Jewish teacher Samson Raphael Hirsch, who said: "The aim of our worship is the purification, enlightenment and uplifting of our inner selves. . . . Its aim is not simply to stir up the emotions, or to produce a fleeting moment of devotion, but the cleansing of heart and mind." **3**

This beautiful meditation, which comes
after the end of the *Tefillah*, also goes back
to Talmud times (Berachot 17).

CLOSING MEDITATION

נְצֹר לְשׁוֹנִי מֵרָע

אֱלֹהַי, נְצֹר לְשׁוֹנִי מֵרָע,
וּשְׂפָתַי מִדַּבֵּר מִרְמָה.
וְלִמְקַלְלַי נַפְשִׁי תִדֹּם,
וְנַפְשִׁי כֶּעָפָר לַכֹּל תִּהְיֶה.
פְּתַח לִבִּי בְּתוֹרָתֶךָ,
וּבְמִצְוֹתֶיךָ תִּרְדֹּף נַפְשִׁי.
וְכָל־הַחוֹשְׁבִים עָלַי רָעָה,
מְהֵרָה הָפֵר עֲצָתָם
וְקַלְקֵל מַחֲשַׁבְתָּם.
עֲשֵׂה לְמַעַן שְׁמֶךָ, עֲשֵׂה לְמַעַן
יְמִינֶךָ, עֲשֵׂה לְמַעַן קְדֻשָּׁתֶךָ,
עֲשֵׂה לְמַעַן תּוֹרָתֶךָ.
לְמַעַן יֵחָלְצוּן יְדִידֶיךָ,
הוֹשִׁיעָה יְמִינְךָ וַעֲנֵנִי.
יִהְיוּ לְרָצוֹן אִמְרֵי פִי, וְהֶגְיוֹן
לִבִּי לְפָנֶיךָ, יְיָ צוּרִי וְגֹאֲלִי.
עֹשֶׂה שָׁלוֹם בִּמְרוֹמָיו, הוּא
יַעֲשֶׂה שָׁלוֹם עָלֵינוּ וְעַל
כָּל־יִשְׂרָאֵל, וְאִמְרוּ אָמֵן.

O God, guard my tongue from evil,
and my lips from deceit.
Let me be silent even to those who
curse me:
Let my spirit be uncontentious like
the dust.
Open my heart to Your Torah, and
let my soul pursue Your *mitzvot*.
If any design evil against me,
rebuff their plan speedily,
and frustrate their design.
Do this for the sake of Your name,
for Your power, for Your
holiness, Your Torah:
That Your loved ones be delivered,
let Your right hand save and
answer me.
May the words of my mouth and
the meditation of my heart be
acceptable to you, Lord,
my Rock and my Redeemer.
May He who establishes peace in
the heavens above, establish
peace for all of us and for all
Israel, and say you: Amen.

1 נְצֹר לְשׁוֹנִי — GUARD MY TONGUE: This meditation, in contrast to the communal spirit of the *Tefillah*, is personal to each worshiper. David Abudarham (14th century) said of this: "Though the choice of good or evil is in the hands of man, yet he entreats God to help him in choosing the good."

2 אִמְרֵי פִי — THE WORDS MY HEART: Before the *Tefillah* begins, the worshiper recites a verse silently (Psalm 51:17) to establish the mood (see p. 49). In concluding, the present verse (Psalm 19:15) is also recited silently.

3 עֹשֶׂה שָׁלוֹם — MAY HE WHO ESTABLISHES PEACE: This phrase is familiar as the last sentence of the full *Kaddish*.

The basic Shabbat passage from
Genesis is repeated.

VAICHULU

וַיְכֻלּוּ

Genesis 2:1-3

1 וַיְכֻלּוּ הַשָּׁמַיִם וְהָאָרֶץ
וְכָל־צְבָאָם.
2 וַיְכַל אֱלֹהִים בַּיּוֹם הַשְּׁבִיעִי
3 מְלַאכְתּוֹ אֲשֶׁר עָשָׂה,
וַיִּשְׁבֹּת בַּיּוֹם הַשְּׁבִיעִי
מִכָּל־מְלַאכְתּוֹ אֲשֶׁר עָשָׂה.
וַיְבָרֶךְ אֱלֹהִים אֶת־יוֹם הַשְּׁבִיעִי
וַיְקַדֵּשׁ אֹתוֹ,
4 כִּי בוֹ שָׁבַת מִכָּל־מְלַאכְתּוֹ
אֲשֶׁר בָּרָא אֱלֹהִים לַעֲשׂוֹת.

1 Heaven and earth were complete,
with all their array.
On the seventh day God completed
the work He had done.
He rested on the seventh day from
all the work He had done.
And God blessed the seventh day
and sanctified it,
for on this day God ceased from all
the work of creation that He
had done.

וַיְכֻלּוּ הַשָּׁמַיִם וְהָאָרֶץ — HEAVEN AND EARTH WERE COMPLETE: These verses
(Genesis 2:1-3), already recited in the *Tefillah*, are repeated here, and are repeated
again, traditionally, as a foreword to the *Kiddush* (blessing on wine) at home to
become a threefold reminder of how Shabbat began. | 1

בַּיּוֹם הַשְּׁבִיעִי — ON THE SEVENTH DAY: This passage reminds us that Shabbat
was God's day of rest on the seventh day of the creation. But the major emphasis is
on the miracle of creation itself. We cannot visualize God "resting"; still, the
thought of His "rest" and of its relationship to our own day of rest is a unique
delight which we enjoy intimately. The miracle of creation, however, is of a different order: it is the reality on which the universe and human existence are based. It,
too, cannot be visualized in human terms; but it is absorbed as a rock of belief,
without which Judaism would be baseless. To explain creation as a metaphor, or to
present it in quasi-scientific terms—as some well-meaning theologians try to do—
is to obfuscate the miracle. The rabbis saw it as "reality," even if they then pro-
ceeded to weave fantasies about it. | 2

מְלַאכְתּוֹ אֲשֶׁר עָשָׂה — THE WORK HE HAD DONE: A high point in rabbinic talk
of creation was the role of the Torah. The Rabbis argued that God's moral aim for
man, as expressed in the Torah, was His whole purpose in creating the universe. In
one form of this argument, God created the Torah at a very early stage, and then
consulted it as to how He was to complete the world. Lightheartedly, the Rabbis
said that the letters of the Hebrew alphabet also played a direct part in creation,
competing with each other to have the honor of being the first letter to appear in
the Torah. | 3

מִכָּל־מְלַאכְתּוֹ אֲשֶׁר בָּרָא אֱלֹהִים לַעֲשׂוֹת — ALL THE WORK OF CREATION THAT
HE HAD DONE: Traditionally, man is central to God's purpose in creation. This
accounts for the bitterness in a poem called "Psalm" by Paul Celan (1920–72): "No
one kneads us again of earth and clay / No one incants our dust / No one." | 4

66

A summary of the seven
blessings of the *Tefillah*

BERACHAH ME'EN SHEVA

בְּרָכָה מֵעֵין שֶׁבַע

בָּרוּךְ אַתָּה יְיָ, אֱלֹהֵינוּ וֵאלֹהֵי אֲבוֹתֵינוּ, אֱלֹהֵי אַבְרָהָם, אֱלֹהֵי יִצְחָק, וֵאלֹהֵי יַעֲקֹב, הָאֵל הַגָּדֹל הַגִּבּוֹר וְהַנּוֹרָא, אֵל עֶלְיוֹן, קוֹנֵה שָׁמַיִם וָאָרֶץ.	1 2	Be blessed, O Lord our God and the God of our Fathers, The God of Abraham, the God of Isaac, and the God of Jacob; God who is great, mighty and awesome, God supreme, the founder of heaven and earth.
מָגֵן אָבוֹת בִּדְבָרוֹ, מְחַיֵּה מֵתִים בְּמַאֲמָרוֹ. הָאֵל הַקָּדוֹשׁ שֶׁאֵין כָּמוֹהוּ, הַמֵּנִיחַ לְעַמּוֹ בְּיוֹם שַׁבַּת קָדְשׁוֹ. כִּי בָם רָצָה לְהָנִיחַ לָהֶם, לְפָנָיו נַעֲבֹד בְּיִרְאָה וָפַחַד, וְנוֹדֶה לִשְׁמוֹ בְּכָל־יוֹם תָּמִיד מֵעֵין הַבְּרָכוֹת.	3	His word was a shield to our fathers; By His will, the spirit of man is eternal. God who is holy, unique in the universe, Who gives rest to His people Israel on His holy Sabbath. It was through his favor that a Sabbath of rest came to them; We serve Him with awe and reverence, and give thanks to His name every day, continuously, In this flow of blessings.

1 וֵאלֹהֵי אֲבוֹתֵינוּ — GOD OF OUR FATHERS: This brief recapitulation of the Shabbat evening *Tefillah* opens, like the *Tefillah,* with the invocation of "God of our Fathers."

2 אֵל עֶלְיוֹן — GOD SUPREME: *El Elyon* is an archaic name for God, dating back to ancient Canaan. In the Tell el-Amarna Letters (15th–14th century B.C.E.) *El Elyon* indicates the Lord of the gods. In Genesis 14:18, Abraham makes a peace treaty with Malkitzedek, King of Salem (perhaps Jerusalem), who is described as "the priest of El Elyon." In replying to Malkitzedek (Genesis 14:22), Abraham uses the same term but defines the Hebrew God as "Creator of Heaven and Earth." The late professor Louis Hartman commented: "Whereas for the pagan, the term referred to the god who was supreme over the other gods, in Israel it referred to the transcendent nature of the one true God."

3 בְּיִרְאָה וָפַחַד — WITH AWE AND REVERENCE: The Hebrew *pahad* ("reverence") appears in Genesis 31:42 as a name of God linked to Isaac: *pahad yitzhak* ("the Revered One of Isaac") which suggests some incident connected with Isaac now lost to memory.

<table>
<tr>
<td>

אֵל הַהוֹדָאוֹת, אֲדוֹן הַשָּׁלוֹם,
מְקַדֵּשׁ הַשַּׁבָּת וּמְבָרֵךְ שְׁבִיעִי,
וּמֵנִיחַ בִּקְדֻשָּׁה
לְעַם מְדֻשְּׁנֵי עֹנֶג,   1
זֵכֶר לְמַעֲשֵׂה בְרֵאשִׁית.

אֱלֹהֵינוּ וֵאלֹהֵי אֲבוֹתֵינוּ,
רְצֵה בִמְנוּחָתֵנוּ.   2
קַדְּשֵׁנוּ בְּמִצְוֹתֶיךָ,
וְתֵן חֶלְקֵנוּ בְּתוֹרָתֶךָ.   3
שַׂבְּעֵנוּ מִטּוּבֶךָ,
וְשַׂמְּחֵנוּ בִּישׁוּעָתֶךָ,

</td>
<td>

God of thanksgiving, Lord of peace,
He sanctified the Sabbath and
  blessed the seventh day;
In holiness, He gives rest to a
  people, full of delight,
To bring creation to our minds.

Our God, God of our Fathers, may
  our rest be pleasing to You.
Sanctify us with Your *mitzvot*, let the
  Torah be our way of life.
Satisfy us with Your goodness,
  gladden us with Your salvation.

</td>
</tr>
</table>

מְדֻשְּׁנֵי עֹנֶג — FULL OF DELIGHT: *Oneg* ("delight") is the most evocative word in the whole celebration of Shabbat. The phrase *medushnei oneg* means literally "fattened with delight," which brings to mind, at one level, the joy of the Shabbat meal. But it is fair to say that it is the special aura of Shabbat, and not just the food, which has always gone deep into the Jewish soul. One is reminded of the midrash which asks how light could have been created on the first day, while the sun and moon were not created until the fourth day. The light of the first day was not "worldly" but heavenly—"a light sown for the righteous" (Psalm 97:11). Something unearthly like this was felt for the delight of Shabbat.

רְצֵה בִמְנוּחָתֵנוּ — MAY OUR REST BE PLEASING TO YOU: This calls to mind the mention in the *Tefillah—retzeh*—which talks of the "pleasure" that God derived from the sacrificial worship in the Temple. But this passage then moves forward to God's pleasure when He saw the *mitzvot*, His moral code, observed in the same spirit.

וְתֵן חֶלְקֵנוּ בְּתוֹרָתֶךָ — LET THE TORAH BE OUR WAY OF LIFE: Jews are aware of many ways in which the meaning of this phrase is expressed. One thinks of living by a code of moral conduct based on sentences in the Torah demanding truth and consideration in all dealings with one's fellow humans. The Torah's code of moral conduct includes not just the Ten Commandments but the ideals of absolute honesty, care for the poor, treating one's neighbor as oneself—adding up to the Torah's concept of holiness: "you shall be holy, for I the Lord your God am holy" (Leviticus 19:2). Later, the prophets and then the Rabbis expanded these moral injunctions to form a total framework for man as a moral being. (See the commentary which follows.)

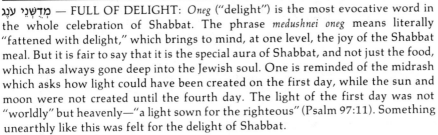

וְטַהֵר לִבֵּנוּ לְעָבְדְּךָ בָּאֱמֶת.	1	Purify our hearts to serve You truthfully.
וְהַנְחִילֵנוּ יְיָ אֱלֹהֵינוּ בְּאַהֲבָה וּבְרָצוֹן שַׁבַּת קָדְשֶׁךָ, וְיָנוּחוּ בָהּ יִשְׂרָאֵל מְקַדְּשֵׁי שְׁמֶךָ.		Let Your holy Sabbath be our heritage, O Lord our God, In love and favor; May all Israel, who sanctify Your name, find rest in it.
בָּרוּךְ אַתָּה יְיָ, מְקַדֵּשׁ הַשַּׁבָּת.	2	Be blessed, O Lord, who sanctifies the Sabbath.

1 לְעָבְדְּךָ בָּאֱמֶת — TO SERVE YOU TRUTHFULLY: The *mitzvot*, the "commandments," of the Torah are a framework for the good life. This is the theme of the first psalm: "Blessed is the man that walks not in the counsel of the ungodly nor stands in the way of sinners, nor sits in the seat of the scornful. . . . He shall be like a tree planted by the rivers of water that brings forth its fruit in its season."

But the Torah as a way of life has always been more than a set of moral principles. Absorption in the Torah is itself uplifting—transforming. A Jew hearing the Torah read in the synagogue hears the echoes of history and faith without having to understand the literal meaning of each sentence. At another level, it is precisely the *study* of the Torah—the search for meaning—which lifts up the spirit of the Jew and has done so for endless centuries.

There is yet another sense in which the Torah is a way of life. The laws which the rabbis drew from the Torah demanded strict obedience in every area of human activity, so that a Jew "obeying the law" felt that he expressed his Jewish faith at every moment, whether the purpose of the law was abstruse or obvious. One didn't evaluate "the laws"; one lived by them as a way of life.

This took the Jew into a love for the Torah which was beyond all reasoning and was mystical in its power. That mystical love is expressed most poetically in a midrash which describes the unearthly mystery of the revelation on Sinai: When God revealed the Torah, no bird sang, no fowl beat its wings, no ox bellowed, the angels did not sing their songs of praise, the sea did not roar, no creature uttered a sound; the world was silent and still, waiting for the echoless divine voice which proclaimed: "I am the Lord your God."

2 מְקַדֵּשׁ הַשַּׁבָּת — WHO SANCTIFIES THE SABBATH: As always in the Shabbat prayers, we are asked to see beyond the happiness that rest gives in the human sense, and to recognize the quality of holiness which flows into life for those who "sanctify Your name," and worship Him as the Being who "sanctified the Sabbath." The concept of *kedushah* ("holiness") which echoed throughout the *Tefillah,* is now repeated in the final blessing of this summary of the *Tefillah.* It is appropriate that what immediately follows is the recital of the *Kaddish*—"Extolled and sanctified be the great the name of God."

69

We read the *Kaddish* in various forms in
every service of worship. Here the full *Kaddish*
is recited by the reader to signal
the end of a section.

KADDISH SHALEM

קַדִּישׁ שָׁלֵם

יִתְגַּדַּל וְיִתְקַדַּשׁ שְׁמֵהּ רַבָּא	1
בְּעָלְמָא דִּי בְרָא כִרְעוּתֵהּ.	2
וְיַמְלִיךְ מַלְכוּתֵהּ	
בְּחַיֵּיכוֹן וּבְיוֹמֵיכוֹן	
וּבְחַיֵּי דְכָל־בֵּית יִשְׂרָאֵל,	
בַּעֲגָלָא וּבִזְמַן קָרִיב,	
וְאִמְרוּ אָמֵן.	

יְהֵא שְׁמֵהּ רַבָּא מְבָרַךְ,
לְעָלַם וּלְעָלְמֵי עָלְמַיָּא.

יִתְבָּרַךְ וְיִשְׁתַּבַּח וְיִתְפָּאַר,
וְיִתְרוֹמַם וְיִתְנַשֵּׂא, וְיִתְהַדָּר
וְיִתְעַלֶּה וְיִתְהַלַּל שְׁמֵהּ דְּקֻדְשָׁא,
בְּרִיךְ הוּא,
לְעֵלָּא מִן כָּל־בִּרְכָתָא וְשִׁירָתָא
תֻּשְׁבְּחָתָא וְנֶחֱמָתָא
דַּאֲמִירָן בְּעָלְמָא,
וְאִמְרוּ אָמֵן.

Extolled and sanctified be the great
name of God
In the world He created by His will.
May He establish His kingdom
during your life, and during
your days, and in the life of
all the House of Israel,
speedily and soon,
and say you: Amen.

May His great name be blessed
forever and ever.

Blessed, praised, glorified, exalted,
extolled and honored,
magnified and lauded be the name
of the Holy One,
Blessed be He.
Though He be high above all
blessings and hymns,
praises and consolations that are
uttered in this world,
and say you: Amen.

Yehei shemei rabba mevarach, le'alam ul'almei almaya.

KADDISH: Different forms of the *Kaddish* are explained in a note on p. 48. In
origin, it expressed the feeling of grace after a period of Torah study, which brings
holiness into daily life.

יִתְגַּדַּל וְיִתְקַדַּשׁ — EXTOLLED AND SANCTIFIED: These opening words of the [1]
Kaddish have a powerful solemnity, evoking the ineffable majesty of God, the
Creator of the universe and the source of the spirit which flows through all of us.
We are humbled but at the same time exalted to be aware of His presence.

כִרְעוּתֵהּ — BY HIS WILL: The universe did not come into existence by accident; it [2]
is an expression of God's will and purpose. Science explains the processes of nature
and the *evolution* of mankind; it cannot explain the *origin* of the universe or the *spirit*
which fills humanity.

תִּתְקַבַּל צְלוֹתְהוֹן וּבָעוּתְהוֹן דְּכָל־בֵּית יִשְׂרָאֵל, קֳדָם אֲבוּהוֹן דְּבִשְׁמַיָּא, וְאִמְרוּ אָמֵן.	May the prayers and supplications of the House of Israel be accepted by their Father in heaven, and say you: Amen.
יְהֵא שְׁלָמָא רַבָּא מִן שְׁמַיָּא וְחַיִּים עָלֵינוּ וְעַל כָּל־יִשְׂרָאֵל, וְאִמְרוּ אָמֵן.	May there be abundant peace from heaven, and life for us and for all Israel; and say you: Amen.
עוֹשֶׂה שָׁלוֹם בִּמְרוֹמָיו, הוּא יַעֲשֶׂה שָׁלוֹם עָלֵינוּ וְעַל כָּל־יִשְׂרָאֵל, וְאִמְרוּ אָמֵן.	May He who establishes peace in the heavens above, establish peace for all of us and for all Israel, and say you: Amen.

1 צְלוֹתְהוֹן וּבָעוּתְהוֹן — PRAYERS AND SUPPLICATIONS: This reference to prayers is included only in the *Kaddish* which immediately follows the *Tefillah*.

2 אֲבוּהוֹן דְּבִשְׁמַיָּא — THEIR FATHER IN HEAVEN: In his book *A Jewish Theology*, Louis Jacobs says that the term "Father" for God is generally used in the rabbinic literature with the pronominal suffix meaning "our." The frequent combination, "Our Father who is in Heaven," serves to make the divine name more abstract and impersonal. (The Christian *Lord's Prayer*—"Our Father who art in Heaven, hallowed be Thy name"—is, of course, a clear echo of rabbinical prayer.)

3 יְהֵא שְׁלָמָא רַבָּא — MAY THERE BE ABUNDANT PEACE: The late Rabbi David de Sola Pool wrote, in his book on the *Kaddish*, that this phrase "seems to have grown out of an original greeting of peace. The congregation would part with the mutual word *shalom* [then, as now, a common term of Jewish salutation] which in the course of time became incorporated in the *Kaddish* itself."

4 עוֹשֶׂה שָׁלוֹם — MAY HE WHO ESTABLISHES PEACE: This sentence, which is in Hebrew, is close in meaning to the previous sentence, in Aramaic. Rabbi Pool thought that one aim of the repetition was to ensure that the *Kaddish* ended with the idea of *shalom*. We saw earlier (p. 65) that the same prayer for peace is added to the silent prayer following the *Tefillah*. We are familiar with it, also, as part of the conclusion of the *Birkat Hamazon* (the "Grace after Meals"). It is a very old custom that when this sentence is recited, the worshiper takes three steps backward, with respectful bows. This was the way the priests and Levites retired from "the Presence" after the service in the Temple (Babylonian Talmud, *Yoma* 53a).

The ceremony sanctifying Shabbat with a
blessing over a cup of wine is an endearing
Jewish tradition, with many
historical overtones.

KIDDUSH

קִדּוּשׁ

בָּרוּךְ אַתָּה יְיָ אֱלֹהֵינוּ מֶלֶךְ הָעוֹלָם, בּוֹרֵא פְּרִי הַגָּפֶן. **1**	Be blessed, Lord our God, King of the Universe, who has created the fruit of the vine.
בָּרוּךְ אַתָּה יְיָ אֱלֹהֵינוּ מֶלֶךְ הָעוֹלָם, אֲשֶׁר קִדְּשָׁנוּ בְּמִצְוֹתָיו וְרָצָה בָנוּ, וְשַׁבַּת קָדְשׁוֹ בְּאַהֲבָה וּבְרָצוֹן הִנְחִילָנוּ, זִכָּרוֹן לְמַעֲשֵׂה בְרֵאשִׁית. כִּי הוּא יוֹם תְּחִלָּה לְמִקְרָאֵי קֹדֶשׁ, זֵכֶר לִיצִיאַת מִצְרָיִם. **2** **3**	Be blessed, Lord our God, King of the Universe, who has sanctified us with His *mitzvot* and shown us His favor. With love and favor, He gave us the holiness of Sabbath as an inheritance, to bring Creation to our minds. It is first among our sacred days, reminding us of the Exodus from Egypt.

פְּרִי הַגָּפֶן — FRUIT OF THE VINE: In biblical times, the Holy Land was famed for its wine. Some scholars (e.g., W. F. Albright) believe that father Abraham was a merchant whose caravans carried wine to Egypt for sale there. The men sent by Moses "to spy out the land" brought back with them "a branch with one cluster of grapes, and they bore it between two upon a staff" (Numbers 13:23). The Promised Land was not simply "a land flowing with milk and honey" but was fertile also in corn, wine and oil (Deuteronomy 7:13). The psalmist, rejoicing in God's manifold bounty, thanks Him "for wine that maketh glad the heart of man" (Psalm 104:15). **1**

בְּמִצְוֹתָיו — WITH HIS MITZVOT: Wine was always used in ceremonials, going back to the Temple offerings described in the Bible (Numbers 28). We all know of the obligatory four cups of wine that everyone—family or strangers—is given as part of the Passover Seder. The Jews were fully aware of the dangers of excess, described so graphically in Proverbs: "Wine is a mocker, strong drink is raging; and whosoever is deceived thereby is not wise" (Proverbs 20:1). But wine has always been enjoyed; and the moment of raising the cup of wine in blessing is always a happy moment in the ritual. **2**

זֵכֶר לִיצִיאַת מִצְרָיִם — REMINDING US OF THE EXODUS FROM EGYPT: Just as Shabbat highlights the miracle of creation, so does it highlight the Exodus, the key event in Jewish history, leading directly to the Revelation on Mount Sinai. The link between these momentous, miraculous events is that observance of Shabbat was given as one of the Ten Commandments at Sinai. **3**

כִּי בָנוּ בָחַרְתָּ וְאוֹתָנוּ קִדַּשְׁתָּ	1	For You have chosen and sanctified us among all nations;
מִכָּל־הָעַמִּים,	2	
וְשַׁבַּת קָדְשְׁךָ בְּאַהֲבָה וּבְרָצוֹן הִנְחַלְתָּנוּ.	3	In love and favor You have given us Your holy Sabbath as an inheritance.
בָּרוּךְ אַתָּה יְיָ, מְקַדֵּשׁ הַשַּׁבָּת.		Blessed be the Lord, who sanctifies the Sabbath.

1 בָנוּ בָחַרְתָּ — YOU HAVE CHOSEN US: To talk of the Jews as "the chosen people" is not a boast but an expression of duty. Moses tells Israel (Deuteronomy 14:2) that God has chosen them as "His own" and commanded them to follow the Torah with its moral duties (Deuteronomy 26:16). If they walk in God's ways, he says (Deuteronomy 26:19), they will be "a holy people unto God," and in this sense "high above all nations."

2 מִכָּל־הָעַמִּים — FROM AMONG ALL NATIONS: The sense of privilege in this phrase is that of standing in close relationship to God's Torah in order to fulfill the *mitzvot*. This privilege does not arise because God chose the Jews, but because the Jews alone "of all the nations" chose God. David Goldstein's *Jewish Folklore and Legend* offers rabbinic tales of this magic scene:

"The Torah was given publicly and openly, in a place to which no one had any claim. For if it had been given in the land of Israel, the nations of the world could have said: We have no portion in it. Therefore it was given in the wilderness, publicly and openly, and in a place to which no one had any claim. Everyone who desires to accept it, let him come and accept it. (*Melchilta Yitro*)

"Although the Torah is written in Hebrew, God actually declaimed it at Sinai in seventy different languages, at one and the same time so that all the inhabitants of the world could hear it and accept it. (Babylonian Talmud, *Shabbat* 88b)

"But they did not do so. When they were asked whether they could obey God's law, they inquired as to its contents. One by one they refused. The descendants of Esau said that they could not live by the commandment "thou shalt not kill"; the descendants of Ishmael could not promise to observe the precept "thou shalt not steal"; and all the other nations hesitated in a similar way.

"Israel was the last nation left, but they did not ask first what the Torah contained. They immediately replied: We shall observe it." (*Sifre* on Deuteronomy)

3 הִנְחַלְתָּנוּ — YOU HAVE GIVEN US . . . AS AN INHERITANCE: In Jewish *theology*, all mankind are equally children of God . In Jewish *history*, there has been an awareness among Jews of a special identity, which has brought with it both suffering and pride. The suffering need not be spelled out; the pride takes one form in the happiness of kinship. Faith in God was a starting point of the Jews' sense of unity as a "family."

There is a unique majesty in the *Alenu* prayer.
The service is coming to an end. We need
words to express the meaning of this
experience—to make it vivid and lasting.

ALENU

עָלֵינוּ

עָלֵינוּ לְשַׁבֵּחַ לַאֲדוֹן הַכֹּל, לָתֵת גְּדֻלָּה לְיוֹצֵר בְּרֵאשִׁית. שֶׁלֹּא עָשָׂנוּ כְּגוֹיֵי הָאֲרָצוֹת, וְלֹא שָׂמָנוּ כְּמִשְׁפְּחוֹת הָאֲדָמָה.	1	It is our duty to praise the Lord of all things, To ascribe greatness to the Creator That He has not made us like the nations of other lands,
שֶׁלֹּא שָׂם חֶלְקֵנוּ כָּהֶם, וְגוֹרָלֵנוּ כְּכָל־הֲמוֹנָם.	2	And not placed us like the other families of earth: Our inheritance is different from theirs, our role on earth has been separate;
וַאֲנַחְנוּ כֹּרְעִים וּמִשְׁתַּחֲוִים וּמוֹדִים לִפְנֵי מֶלֶךְ מַלְכֵי הַמְּלָכִים, הַקָּדוֹשׁ בָּרוּךְ הוּא.	3	For we bend the knee and offer worship and thanks to the Supreme king of kings, The Holy One, blessed be He.

Alenu leshabe-aḥ la'adon hakol, latet gedulah leyotzer
bereshit. Shelo asanu kegoyei ha'aratzot, velo samanu
kemishpeḥot ha'adamah. Shelo sam ḥelkenu kahem
vegoralenu kechol hamonam. Va'anaḥnu kor'im umishtaḥavim
umodim lifne melech malchei hamelachim, hakadosh
baruch hu.

עָלֵינוּ — IT IS OUR DUTY: The *Alenu* prayer has a unique solemnity. It was originally composed for the Rosh Hashanah (New Year) service, and is a central feature
of that section of the service known as *Malchuyot*—God as King. Its expressiveness
as a prayer was felt so deeply that it was made the concluding prayer for all our
services of worship. It is in two sections: in the first, we look into our hearts as
Jews; in the second, we consider mankind as a whole.

שֶׁלֹּא שָׂם חֶלְקֵנוּ כָּהֶם, וְגוֹרָלֵנוּ כְּכָל־הֲמוֹנָם — OUR INHERITANCE IS DIFFERENT
FROM THEIRS, OUR ROLE ON EARTH HAS BEEN SEPARATE: In this first
section of *Alenu*, we face our distinctiveness as Jews, and try to understand it. God,
Creator of the universe, "has not made us like the nations of other lands." Because
of the Revelation at Mount Sinai, Jews have had an abiding purpose for existence:
to proclaim God's greatness and eternity, His majesty, His omnipotence. Remem-
bering this, as our service ends, we are seeing God through our eyes as Jews.

וַאֲנַחְנוּ כֹּרְעִים וּמִשְׁתַּחֲוִים — FOR WE BEND THE KNEE AND OFFER WORSHIP:
In very old versions of *Alenu*, the contrast between Judaism and paganism was
highlighted by a sentence at this point which said that others "bow down to vanity
and emptiness, and pray to a god that saves not"—a contrast to the Jewish worship
of the true God. This sentence was dropped when it was asserted—quite falsely—
that the words were intended as a sneer at Christians. *Alenu* goes back, in fact, to a
pre-Christian era.

שֶׁהוּא נוֹטֶה שָׁמַיִם
וְיֹסֵד אָרֶץ,
וּמוֹשַׁב יְקָרוֹ בַּשָּׁמַיִם מִמַּעַל,
וּשְׁכִינַת עֻזּוֹ
בְּגָבְהֵי מְרוֹמִים.
הוּא אֱלֹהֵינוּ, אֵין עוֹד,
אֱמֶת מַלְכֵּנוּ, אֶפֶס זוּלָתוֹ.
כַּכָּתוּב בְּתוֹרָתוֹ :
וְיָדַעְתָּ הַיּוֹם וַהֲשֵׁבֹתָ אֶל לְבָבֶךָ,
כִּי יְיָ הוּא הָאֱלֹהִים
בַּשָּׁמַיִם מִמַּעַל
וְעַל הָאָרֶץ מִתָּחַת,
אֵין עוֹד.

1 He stretched out the heavens and
laid the foundations of the
earth;
2 The seat of His splendor is in the
heavens above: the abode of His
might in the loftiest heights.
He is our God, there is no other;
He is our king in truth, beyond
compare;
And so it is written in His Torah:
"Know this day, and take it to your
heart
3 That the Lord is God, in the heavens
above and on the earth below;
There is no other."

1 שֶׁהוּא נוֹטֶה שָׁמַיִם — HE STRETCHED OUT THE HEAVENS: This passage on the majesty of creation leads us from the first section of *Alenu*, dealing with our feeling as Jews, to the second section, with its universalist prayer for mankind.

2 בַּשָּׁמַיִם מִמַּעַל . . . בְּגָבְהֵי מְרוֹמִים — IN THE HEAVENS ABOVE . . . IN THE LOFTIEST HEIGHTS: The worshiper tries, inadequately, to find words to describe the mystery of Infinity which is involved in the concept of God. The rabbis expressed this obliquely in one of the names they applied to God—*makom* ("the Place"), by which they meant the Being who expresses the infinity of space. One rabbi said on this: "Why do we call God *makom*? Because He is the place of His world, but this [limited] world is not His [only] place." These concepts were explored poetically in the *hechalot* hymns, composed by *merkavah* mystics in the third and fourth centuries. The hymns centered on the seven heavenly "palaces" (*hechalot*) through which the visionary aspires to pass, and "the chariot" throne (*merkavah*) in the innermost palace.

3 אֶל לְבָבֶךָ — TO YOUR HEART: Inevitably, this brings to mind the familiar injunction of the *Sh'ma*, to love God "with all your heart, and all your soul, and all your might." There is a touching saying on the feelings of the heart by the *hasid* Menaḥem Mendel of Rimanov (d. 1815): "Every sorrow that a Jew tells me leaves a mark on my heart; and when I stand up to recite the *Tefillah* I open my heart to God and pray that He may read every sorrow recorded on it."

עַל כֵּן נְקַוֶּה לְךָ יְיָ אֱלֹהֵינוּ	1	Therefore we look in hope to You, O Lord our God,
לִרְאוֹת מְהֵרָה בְּתִפְאֶרֶת עֻזֶּךָ,		That we may soon behold the glory of Your power.
לְהַעֲבִיר גִּלּוּלִים מִן הָאָרֶץ		in which the abominations of the earth will pass away,
וְהָאֱלִילִים כָּרוֹת יִכָּרֵתוּן,	2	and the false idols of mankind will be utterly destroyed.

נְקַוֶּה — WE LOOK IN HOPE: The prayer now turns to a vision of what this world will be when mankind is filled with the faith in God that the prophets called for, when, in the words of Isaiah, "the earth shall be full of the knowledge of the Lord as the waters cover the sea" (Isaiah 11:9). It is to be noted that this vision of the perfect existence for mankind is in terms of the realistic life we know on earth, not in terms of the mystical idea of a messianic age, or *olam haba*—the world after death that the fortunate will inherit.

Not that the Jews fought shy of creating delightful fantasies of a world to come that will wipe out, as it were, the suffering and injustice of the world we know. In the view of the famous third-century rabbi known as "Rav," the joys of paradise were, so to speak, out of this world: "There is neither eating nor drinking, nor any begetting of children, no bargaining or jealousy or hatred or strife. All that the righteous do is to sit with their crowns on their heads and enjoy the effulgence of the divine Presence."

But none of this was serious or important, compared with the saintly life as lived on earth. A rabbi quoted in *Pirkei Avot* ("Ethics of the Fathers") 4:17 expressed the idea as follows: "One moment of repentance and good deeds in this world is better than the entire life of the world to come."

וְהָאֱלִילִים כָּרוֹת יִכָּרֵתוּן — AND THE FALSE IDOLS OF MANKIND WILL BE UTTERLY DESTROYED: In the perfect world that Jews pray for in *Alenu*, the distinction between Jew and pagan will have disappeared. It is to be a world devoid of enmity, symbolized by a new harmony in nature itself: "the wolf shall dwell with the lamb, and the leopard shall lie down with the kid." In a different approach to "the world to come," the Kabbalah of Isaac Luria (1534–1572) explains that three cosmic processes comprise the transformation. The first was *tzimtzum* ("contraction"), in which God, originally "all in all," contracted Himself to leave a vacuum for Creation, a continuous process. The second stage introduced evil, the shattering of the heavenly spheres ("breaking of the vessels"), whose shards still reflect some sparks of God's radiance. In the third process, *tikkun*, these sparks are gathered to restore the universe to perfection, through full observance of the Torah, leading to the messianic age.

לְתַקֵּן עוֹלָם בְּמַלְכוּת שַׁדַּי 1
וְכָל־בְּנֵי בָשָׂר יִקְרְאוּ בִשְׁמֶךָ,
לְהַפְנוֹת אֵלֶיךָ כָּל־רִשְׁעֵי־אָרֶץ.
יַכִּירוּ וְיֵדְעוּ כָּל־יוֹשְׁבֵי תֵבֵל
כִּי לְךָ תִּכְרַע כָּל־בֶּרֶךְ,
תִּשָּׁבַע כָּל לָשׁוֹן.
לְפָנֶיךָ יְיָ אֱלֹהֵינוּ יִכְרְעוּ וְיִפֹּלוּ,
וְלִכְבוֹד שִׁמְךָ יְקָר יִתֵּנוּ,
וִיקַבְּלוּ כֻלָם אֶת־עֹל מַלְכוּתֶךָ, 2

It is our dream that the world be perfected
under the kingdom of the Almighty, and all humanity will call Your name;
forsaking evil, all will turn to You.
All who live on earth will come together and know
that to You alone every knee must bend,
every tongue swear allegiance.
To You, O Lord our God, all will bow in humility,
all will give honor to Your glorious Name.
All humanity will accept the yoke of Your kingdom,

---

1 לְתַקֵּן עוֹלָם — THE WORLD WILL BE PERFECTED: The Hebrew means literally: "to restore the world." The verb *tikken* gave rise to the postbiblical word *tikkun*, used in Kabbalah (see previous note) to describe the restoration of the universe to its primeval perfection. This is the theme of a poem by the American poet Howard Schwartz called "Gathering the Sparks":

That is why we were created / to search for the sparks / No matter where they have been / Hidden / And as each one is revealed / to be consumed / in our own fire / And reborn / Out of our own / Ashes

Someday / When the sparks have been gathered / The vessels will be / Restored / And the fleet will set sail / Across another ocean / Of space / And the Word / Will be spoken / Again

2 עֹל מַלְכוּתֶךָ — THE YOKE OF YOUR KINGDOM: This is an unusual metaphor, which prompts some thought. "Yoke" (*ol*, in Hebrew) is mostly used in the Bible to indicate an unwelcome burden, as when Moses tells the Israelites that if they are sinful, God "will put a yoke of iron on your neck" (Deuteronomy 28:48). But in later times, Jews spoke of the "the yoke of the Torah" to indicate something that one carried on one's shoulders, not as a burden but as a guiding force. In this prayer, too, the yoke of God's kingdom denotes a sense of duty and responsibility that will permeate mankind in the perfect age.

וְתִמְלֹךְ עֲלֵיהֶם מְהֵרָה לְעוֹלָם וָעֶד.	1	and You will rule over them speedily, forever and ever.	
כִּי הַמַּלְכוּת שֶׁלְּךָ הִיא,	2	For the kingdom is Yours; and for all eternity You will rule in glory.	
וּלְעוֹלְמֵי עַד תִּמְלֹךְ בְּכָבוֹד.	3		
כַּכָּתוּב בְּתוֹרָתֶךָ:		And thus it is written in Your Torah: "The Lord will reign forever and ever."	
יְיָ יִמְלֹךְ לְעֹלָם וָעֶד.			
וְנֶאֱמַר: וְהָיָה יְיָ לְמֶלֶךְ עַל כָּל־הָאָרֶץ,		And it is said: "The Lord shall be king over the whole earth.	
בַּיּוֹם הַהוּא יִהְיֶה יְיָ אֶחָד וּשְׁמוֹ אֶחָד.	4	On that day, the Lord shall be One, and His Name shall be one."	

וְתִמְלֹךְ — AND YOU WILL RULE: The concept of God as King goes back to the archaic poetry of the Bible, as in the song at the Red Sea that was a shout of happy affirmation: "The Lord will reign forever and ever" (Exodus 15:18).

הַמַּלְכוּת שֶׁלְּךָ הִיא — THE KINGDOM IS YOURS: God as King is the theme of some of the psalms recited at the opening of this service. Psalms 96 to 99 are usually called "enthronement psalms," emphasizing God's royal role in the universe. They offer a contrast to those psalms—often called "the royal psalms"—dealing with the *earthly* king of Israel. But if this earthly king is human, fallible and dependent on God, he is, at the same time, "the anointed one" (*mashiah*) of God, and under His special care. We hear this in the twentieth psalm: "Now I know that the Lord saves His anointed one: He will hear him from His holy Heaven, with the saving strength of His right arm."

תִּמְלֹךְ בְּכָבוֹד — YOU WILL RULE IN GLORY: We need the concept of "glory" to express in words the indefinable power of the Creator; but the Bible stresses equally those concepts of God which make Him the source of our moral ideals: He is a God of justice on the one hand, and mercy on the other. We hear this in the proclamation to Moses on Sinai (Exodus 34:6–7): sin will be punished, but God is "compassionate and gracious, abounding in kindness and faithfulness."

יִהְיֶה יְיָ אֶחָד — THE LORD SHALL BE ONE: The last words of *Alenu* invoke the unity of God with the force of the *Sh'ma*. The verse quoted is a ringing affirmation from Zechariah 14:9. The day will dawn when "the Lord shall be king over the whole earth. On that day, the Lord shall be One and His Name shall be One."

In the midst of bereavement, no words
of reason or explanation can assuage our grief.
Yet we need help, and we find it in the
lyrical solemnity of the *Kaddish*.

KADDISH YATOM

קַדִּישׁ יָתוֹם

יִתְגַּדַּל וְיִתְקַדַּשׁ שְׁמֵהּ רַבָּא 1	Extolled and sanctified be the great name of God
בְּעָלְמָא דִי בְרָא כִרְעוּתֵהּ. 2	In the world He created by His will.
וְיַמְלִיךְ מַלְכוּתֵהּ	May He establish His kingdom
בְּחַיֵּיכוֹן וּבְיוֹמֵיכוֹן	during your life, and during your days, and in the life of all
וּבְחַיֵּי דְכָל־בֵּית יִשְׂרָאֵל,	the House of Israel,
בַּעֲגָלָא וּבִזְמַן קָרִיב,	speedily and soon,
וְאִמְרוּ אָמֵן.	and say you: Amen.
יְהֵא שְׁמֵהּ רַבָּא מְבָרַךְ, 3	May His great name be blessed forever and ever.
לְעָלַם וּלְעָלְמֵי עָלְמַיָּא.	

Yitgaddal veyitkaddash shemei rabba—be'alma divra chir'uteih.
Ve-yamlich malchuteih behayeichon uvyomeichon uvhayei
dechol beit yisra'el, ba'agala uvizman kariv ve'imru amen.

Yehei shemei rabba mevarach, le'alam ul'almei almaya.

KADDISH: We saw earlier (pp. 48 and 70) that the *Kaddish* appears in various forms during the service. Although it is being recited here as a prayer of bereavement, there is no word of death in it. It focuses instead on the force of life within us—the power of life that flows from the Creator. Thoughts of the infinity of God's power in our lives help to assuage the grief of the individual.

1 יִתְגַּדַּל וְיִתְקַדַּשׁ — EXTOLLED AND SANCTIFIED: The *Kaddish* extols God's greatness. The words express the immortality of the soul as part of God's eternity.

2 בְּעָלְמָא דִי בְרָא — IN THE WORLD HE CREATED: Human existence, full of mystery, alternating in happiness and sadness, is central to the world that God brought into being. In the midst of bereavement, we turn to the ancient, hallowed words to acknowledge that we are all part of the world God created.

3 יְהֵא שְׁמֵהּ רַבָּא מְבָרַךְ — MAY HIS GREAT NAME BE BLESSED: This is a response by the whole congregation, assembled, in a united affirmation of God's greatness. The Midrash says of this response that it is the kernel of the *Kaddish*. It echoes the verse in Psalm 113, one of the most beautiful of all psalms:

Praise ye the Lord: Praise, O ye servants of the Lord, Praise the name of the Lord. Blessed be the name of the Lord from this time forth and forevermore. From the rising of the sun unto the going down of the sun, the Lord's name is to be praised.

There is a saying in the Talmud that when this psalm was recited in the Temple, with all those present "joining in loudly and in unison," it had the power of influencing the heavenly decree in one's favor (Babylonian Talmud, *Shabbat* 19b).

יִתְבָּרֵךְ וְיִשְׁתַּבַּח וְיִתְפָּאַר, וְיִתְרוֹמַם וְיִתְנַשֵּׂא, וְיִתְהַדָּר וְיִתְעַלֶּה וְיִתְהַלָּל שְׁמֵהּ דְּקֻדְשָׁא, בְּרִיךְ הוּא, לְעֵלָּא מִן כָּל־בִּרְכָתָא וְשִׁירָתָא תֻּשְׁבְּחָתָא וְנֶחֱמָתָא דַּאֲמִירָן בְּעָלְמָא, וְאִמְרוּ אָמֵן. 1 2 3	Blessed, praised, glorified, exalted, extolled and honored, magnified and lauded be the name of the Holy One, Blessed be He. Though He be high above all blessings and hymns, praises and consolations that are uttered in this world, and say you: Amen.

Yitbarach veyishtabbah veyitpa'ar veyitromam veyitnassei,
veyit-hadar veyit'aleh veyit-halal shemeih dekudshah,
berich hu, le'eila min kol birchata veshirata tushbehata
venehemata da'amiran be'alma ve'imru amen.

יִתְבָּרֵךְ וְיִשְׁתַּבַּח וְיִתְפָּאַר — BLESSED, PRAISED, GLORIFIED: These familiar words help us in our bereavement wherever we recite the *Kaddish*. Normally, this is in our home world, surrounded by friends and loved ones; but its effect is also wider. When we are traveling, the language and ritual of the synagogue we visit may be unfamiliar, but not the *Kaddish*. The *Kaddish* is universal, its mystery uniting us with all our people and all our history. For endless centuries and in every circumstance of living, the same words have risen to God as an affirmation of Jewish existence. We have turned to it to meet sorrow that seems unbearable; Jews who hear the words know that sorrow will be borne.

וְיִתְעַלֶּה וְיִתְהַלָּל — MAGNIFIED AND LAUDED: The intense feeling of the *Kaddish* is paralleled in a poem by Yannai, one of the mystical poets who lived in the Holy Land in the 4th–6th centuries C.E. It ends, after glorifying God, in an ecstatic burst of poetry:

> For You ride on a cherub and fly on a wind:
> Your road is in whirlwind, Your way is in story, Your path is through waters.
> Fires are Your emissaries—thousands and thousands and myriads of myriads,
>   who are changed into men, changed into women, changed into winds,
>   changed into demons
> Who assume all shapes and fulfill every mission with fear, dread, awe,
>   trembling, terror, and trepidation.

תֻּשְׁבְּחָתָא וְנֶחֱמָתָא — PRAISES AND CONSOLATIONS: This one mention of "consolation" is the closest the *Kaddish* gets to reflecting the bereavement of those who recite it. The faith in God expressed in the *Kaddish* is not remote but personal. The words of Isaiah—almost the last words of his vision—speak to us this personal way: "As one whom his mother comforts, so will I comfort you, and in Jerusalem shall you be comforted."

יְהֵא שְׁלָמָא רַבָּא מִן שְׁמַיָּא וְחַיִּים עָלֵינוּ וְעַל כָּל־יִשְׂרָאֵל, וְאִמְרוּ אָמֵן. |1,2

עֹשֶׂה שָׁלוֹם בִּמְרוֹמָיו, הוּא יַעֲשֶׂה שָׁלוֹם עָלֵינוּ וְעַל כָּל־יִשְׂרָאֵל, וְאִמְרוּ אָמֵן. |3

1,2 May there be abundant peace from heaven, and life for us and for all Israel; and say you: Amen.

3 May He who establishes peace in the heavens above, establish peace for all of us and for all Israel, and say you: Amen.

Yehei shelama rabba min shemaya vehayim aleinu ve'al kol yisra'el ve'imru amen.

Oseh shalom bimromav hu ya'aseh shalom aleinu ve'al kol yisra'el ve'imru amen.

---

1 שְׁלָמָא רַבָּא מִן שְׁמַיָּא — ABUNDANT PEACE FROM HEAVEN: We noted earlier in discussing the *Kaddish* that followed the *Tefillah* (p. 71) that the word "peace" (*shelama* in Aramaic; *shalom* in Hebrew) was originally the parting word among people who had studied or prayed together. *Shalom* is more than "peace"; it is a greeting of concern, as when Joseph asks his brothers in the Bible: *hashalom avichem* ("Is your father well?"). But though *shalom* was, and has become again, the universal greeting among Jews, the prayer here is for a reign of peace in the most literal sense, echoed in the final sentence of the *Kaddish*.

2 וְחַיִּים עָלֵינוּ — AND LIFE FOR US: There is a legend about the death of the great Rabbi Akiba, who was martyred by the Romans (c. 135) for his refusal to cease teaching the Torah. The American poet Muriel Rukeyser, who died in 1980, drew on the legend in an emotional poem, "Akiba." It evokes the long, drawn-out death as told in the Midrash. Akiba's flesh "is combed with iron combs," but Akiba is so calm through all this that the Roman commander expresses his astonishment: "What is it? Have you magic powers? Or do you feel no pain?" The poem continues:

> The old man answers, "No. But there is a commandment saying Thou shalt love the Lord thy God with all thy heart, with all thy soul, and with all thy might. I knew that I loved him with all my heart and might. Now I know that I love him with all my life."

3 עֹשֶׂה שָׁלוֹם — HE WHO ESTABLISHES PEACE: Unlike the rest of the *Kaddish*, which is in Aramaic, this final sentence, the prayer for peace, is in Hebrew. We noted earlier that this same prayer for peace is added to the silent prayer following the *Tefillah* (p. 71), and to the Grace after Meals. There are many repetitions of this kind in the prayerbook. As we come to the end of the *Kaddish*, we murmur words that we know well and that never fail to move us.

This beautifully measured hymn may date
back to the Gaonic age (7th–10th centuries);
but some think that the author was the
Spanish-Jewish poet Solomon ibn Gabirol,
(11th century).

ADON OLAM

אֲדוֹן עוֹלָם

<table>
<tr><td>

1 אֲדוֹן עוֹלָם אֲשֶׁר מָלַךְ
2 בְּטֶרֶם כָּל־יְצִיר נִבְרָא,
לְעֵת נַעֲשָׂה בְחֶפְצוֹ כֹּל
אֲזַי מֶלֶךְ שְׁמוֹ נִקְרָא.

וְאַחֲרֵי כִּכְלוֹת הַכֹּל
לְבַדּוֹ יִמְלֹךְ נוֹרָא,
וְהוּא הָיָה וְהוּא הֹוֶה
וְהוּא יִהְיֶה בְּתִפְאָרָה.

3 וְהוּא אֶחָד וְאֵין שֵׁנִי
לְהַמְשִׁיל לוֹ לְהַחְבִּירָה,
בְּלִי רֵאשִׁית בְּלִי תַכְלִית
וְלוֹ הָעֹז וְהַמִּשְׂרָה.

</td><td>

Eternal Lord who reigned before
    any creature was formed—
When at His will all was made, then
    was His Name hailed as King.
When all things shall cease to be,
    He will reign alone, in awe.
He was, He is, He always will exist
    in glory.
He is One, there is no second Being
    to be like unto Him, or at His
    side.
He is without beginning, and
    without end. To Him alone
    belong power and rule.

</td></tr>
</table>

Adon olam asher malach beterem kol yetzir nivra,
L'et na'asah v'hef-tzo kol azai melech shemo nikra.
Ve'aharei kichlot hakol levaddo yimloch nora,
Vehu hayah vehu hoveh vehu yihyeh betif'arah.
Vehu ehad ve'ein sheni lehamshil lo lehahbirah,
Beli reshit beli tachlit velo ha'oz vehamisra.

1 אֲדוֹן עוֹלָם — ETERNAL LORD: This solemn anthem in skillful poetry is an
expression both of the Jewish credo and of intimate personal trust in God.

2 בְּטֶרֶם כָּל־יְצִיר — BEFORE ANY CREATURE: This simple phrase reflects a crucial
difference between Jewish theology and that of the surrounding world at the time
this hymn was written. Aristotle, whose works had been rediscovered, held that
the world and the laws of nature carried eternity with them; in the Jewish view,
the world was created *ex nihilo* by God, and only He expressed infinity and eternity.

3 וְהוּא אֶחָד — HE IS ONE: The unity of God is not numerical but total. Jewish
tradition made this the central idea in the stories of dying for the faith, as in the
martyrdom of Akiba. Akiba, reciting the *Sh'ma* before he died, prolonged the word
ehad ("One") until he expired. In the Rukeyser poem (see p. 81):

    The look of delight of the martyr
    Among the colors of pain, at last knowing his own response
    Total and unified.
    To love God, with all the heart, all passion,
    Every desire called evil, turned toward unity.

וְהוּא אֵלִי וְחַי גֹּאֲלִי | 1
וְצוּר חֶבְלִי בְּעֵת צָרָה,
וְהוּא נִסִּי וּמָנוֹס לִי | 2
מְנָת כּוֹסִי בְּיוֹם אֶקְרָא. | 3

בְּיָדוֹ אַפְקִיד רוּחִי | 4
בְּעֵת אִישָׁן וְאָעִירָה,
וְעִם רוּחִי גְּוִיָּתִי | 5
יְיָ לִי וְלֹא אִירָא.

He is my God, my redeemer lives;
    my rock in times of trouble and
    distress.
He is my banner and my refuge,
The bounty that is mine, on the day
    I call.
Into His hand I entrust my spirit,
    when I sleep and when I wake,
And with my soul, my body also,
    God is with me; I shall not fear.

Vehu eli vehai go'ali vetzur ḥevli be'et tzarah,
Vehu nisi umanos li menat kosi beyom ekra.
Beyado afkid ruḥi be'et ishan ve'a'irah,
Ve'im ruḥi geviyati adonai li velo ira.

---

1   וְחַי גֹּאֲלִי — MY REDEEMER LIVES: This is a conscious quotation of the famous passage in the book of Job (19:25): "I know that my redeemer lives, and that he shall stand at the latter day upon the earth." In biblical Hebrew, go'el (always translated as "redeemer") never had the meaning that it assumed in Christianity as a Being who redeemed man from sin. Go'el usually meant a kinsman who fulfilled the duties of family loyalty and acted as a champion. By extension, it came, in poetry, to mean God, who redeemed one from death.

2   נִסִּי — MY BANNER: The Hebrew word nes ("banner") comes to mean "a sign," and hence "a miracle." There is a suggestion of this in this Adon Olam verse.

3   מְנָת כּוֹסִי — THE BOUNTY THAT IS MINE: Literally, "the portion of my cup." This is an extension, in poetry, of the verse in Psalm 23: ". . . my cup runneth over." The psalmist's cup runs over with bounty from God.

4   בְּיָדוֹ אַפְקִיד רוּחִי — INTO HIS HAND I ENTRUST MY SPIRIT: It is this passage which has made Adon Olam a favorite prayer for reciting before sleep; and by the same token it is a good hymn to sing at the close of the evening service. The skill of the poet, with his steady rhythm—perfectly sustained throughout the hymn—has given this line a superb sense of confidence: "God is with me, I shall not fear."

5   וְעִם רוּחִי גְּוִיָּתִי — AND WITH MY SOUL, MY BODY ALSO: George Foot Moore, in his classical book Judaism, discusses soul and body as the Pharisees saw this subject, in contrast to the Hellenist view of the time. To the Greeks, the soul was separate from the body and imperishable; the Jewish view was of "the unity of man, soul and body."

Yigdal is both a cheerful hymn and a poetic
summation of the creed of Judaism
as set out by Maimonides in his Thirteen
Principles of Faith.

YIGDAL

יִגְדַל

יִגְדַל אֱלֹהִים חַי וְיִשְׁתַּבַּח,
נִמְצָא וְאֵין עֵת אֶל מְצִיאוּתוֹ. |1|

אֶחָד וְאֵין יָחִיד כְּיִחוּדוֹ,
נֶעְלָם וְגַם אֵין סוֹף לְאַחְדוּתוֹ. |2|

אֵין לוֹ דְמוּת הַגּוּף וְאֵינוֹ גוּף,
לֹא נַעֲרֹךְ אֵלָיו קְדֻשָּׁתוֹ. |3| |4|

קַדְמוֹן לְכָל־דָּבָר אֲשֶׁר נִבְרָא,
רִאשׁוֹן וְאֵין רֵאשִׁית לְרֵאשִׁיתוֹ. |5|

Extolled and praised be the living
God. He exists, and His
existence is eternal.
He is One, and there is no unity like
His unity. His "Oneness" is
unfathomable and infinite.
He has no bodily form or substance.
Nothing can compare with His
holiness.
He existed before Creation. He is
the First, but with no beginning
to His beginning.

Yigdal elohim hai veyishtabbah, nimtzah ve'ein et el metzi'uto.
Ehad ve'ein yahid ke-yihudo, ne'lam vegam ein sof le'ahduto.
Ein lo demut haguf ve'eino guf, lo na'aroch elav kedushato.
Kadmon lechol davar asher nivra, rishon ve'ein reshit lereshito.

YIGDAL: Some ascribe this poem to Daniel ben Judah, who lived in Rome in the
first half of the fourteenth century. Others attribute it to a more well known poet,
Immanuel of Rome (c. 1261–c. 1328). Its thirteen lines are double pentameters in a
strict rhythm, with a single rhyme throughout.

נִמְצָא — HE EXISTS: *Yigdal* expresses in verse the "Thirteen Principles" which the |1|
philosopher Maimonides (1135-1204) set out in his Commentary on the Mishnah.
God's eternal existence is the first of the principles.

אֶחָד — HE IS ONE: The insistence on God's unity stood out in contrast to the |2|
Christian doctrine of the trinity.

אֵין לוֹ דְמוּת הַגּוּף — HE HAS NO BODILY FORM: This harks back to the |3|
denunciation of "idols" all through the Bible; but to Jews in a Christian world, it
also reflected a rejection of the images visible everywhere.

לֹא נַעֲרֹךְ — NOTHING CAN COMPARE: No earthly being is imbued with the |4|
holiness that Jews ascribe to God. Even Moses, who "saw" God and heard "his
voice," was human, fallible, and mortal. Nothing can dilute the uniqueness of the
Creator and the sense of awe—holiness—which this inspires.

קַדְמוֹן לְכָל־דָּבָר אֲשֶׁר נִבְרָא — HE EXISTED BEFORE CREATION: This was a |5|
central theme in medieval argument about the nature of God (see note on *Adon
Olam*, p. 82). Aristotle, whose works had been rediscovered, held that the world
and the laws of nature carried eternity with them; in the Jewish view, God created
the world *ex nihilo*. Only He expresses infinity and eternity. He transcends man and
the universe; yet He is also immanent within the world and the human soul.

הִנּוֹ אֲדוֹן עוֹלָם, וְכָל־נוֹצָר ‎1
יוֹרֶה גְדֻלָּתוֹ וּמַלְכוּתוֹ.

שֶׁפַע נְבוּאָתוֹ נְתָנוֹ אֶל ‎2
אַנְשֵׁי סְגֻלָּתוֹ וְתִפְאַרְתּוֹ.

לֹא קָם בְּיִשְׂרָאֵל כְּמֹשֶׁה עוֹד
נָבִיא וּמַבִּיט אֶת־תְּמוּנָתוֹ.

תּוֹרַת אֱמֶת נָתַן לְעַמּוֹ אֵל,

עַל יַד נְבִיאוֹ נֶאֱמַן בֵּיתוֹ. ‎3

לֹא יַחֲלִיף הָאֵל וְלֹא יָמִיר

דָּתוֹ, לְעוֹלָמִים לְזוּלָתוֹ. ‎4

He is the eternal Lord. All that is created expresses his greatness and sovereignty.

He endowed with prophetic insight men of His choice and glory.

No prophet has arisen in Israel like Moses—prophet and close to God's radiance.

God gave His Torah of truth to His people through His prophet Moses, faithful to His house.

God will not alter, nor change His teaching; it is with Him forever.

Hinno adon olam, vechol notzar yoreh gedulato umalchuto.
Shefa nevu'ato netano el anshei segulato vetif-arto.
Lo yahalif ha'el velo yamir dato le'olamim lezulato.
Lo kam be-yisra'el kemosheh od navi umabbit et temunato.
Torat emet natan le'amo el, al yad nevi'o ne'eman beito.

---

1 וְכָל־נוֹצָר — ALL THAT IS CREATED: In the *Ani Ma'amin* ("I Believe") credo, also based on the Thirteen Principles of Maimonides, this fifth principle is expressed with a special emphasis for Jews: "I believe with perfect faith that to the Creator alone is it proper to pray; it is not proper to pray to any other Being."

2 שֶׁפַע נְבוּאָתוֹ — PROPHETIC INSIGHT: *Yigdal*, being in verse, talks of the prophets with much more imagination than *Ani Ma'amin*, which says simply: "I believe with perfect faith that all the words of the prophets are true." In *Yigdal*, the words *shefa nevu'ato* translate literally as "the rich gift of God's own prophecy," with which He endowed these men. The inexplicable quality of genius—like that of Mozart—is similarly a rich gift from God.

3 וּמַבִּיט אֶת־תְּמוּנָתוֹ — CLOSE TO GOD'S RADIANCE: The Hebrew words mean, literally, "he beheld God's likeness," but this is clearly to be taken symbolically. Moses on Sinai is a rich subject for rabbinical storytelling. One comment is that Moses could not have survived on Sinai for forty days and nights without food or drink, and that therefore he must really have gone up to heaven itself, where the angels survive without sustenance. In heaven, the story goes on, the angels tried to prevent Moses from taking the Torah away from them and down to earth; but he persuaded them that mankind needed the Torah more than *they* did!

4 נֶאֱמַן בֵּיתוֹ — FAITHFUL TO HIS HOUSE: The Hebrew *ne'eman* ("faithful") is echoed not just in *emunah* ("faith") but in *amen,* an affirmation of belief.

85

צוֹפֶה וְיוֹדֵעַ סְתָרֵינוּ, 1
מַבִּיט לְסוֹף דָּבָר בְּקַדְמָתוֹ.
גּוֹמֵל לְאִישׁ חֶסֶד כְּמִפְעָלוֹ, 2
נוֹתֵן לְרָשָׁע רַע כְּרִשְׁעָתוֹ.
יִשְׁלַח לְקֵץ יָמִים מְשִׁיחֵנוּ, 3,4
לִפְדּוֹת מְחַכֵּי קֵץ יְשׁוּעָתוֹ.
מֵתִים יְחַיֶּה אֵל בְּרֹב חַסְדּוֹ, 5
בָּרוּךְ עֲדֵי עַד שֵׁם תְּהִלָּתוֹ.

He watches and knows our secret thoughts. He sees the end in its beginning.
He rewards the good deeds of men. The evil-doer suffers for wickedness.
He will send our Messiah at the end of time, to redeem those who wait for the end—His salvation.
Through His love, He renews life beyond death. Blessed forever-more be His glorious Name.

Tzofeh ve-yodea setareinu, mabbit lesof davar bekadmato.
Gomel le'ish ḥesed kemif-alo, noten lerasha ra kerish-ato.
Yishlaḥ leketz yamim meshiḥenu, lifdot meḥakkei ketz yeshu'ato.
Metim yeḥayeh el berov ḥasdo, baruch addei ad shem tehillato.

צוֹפֶה וְיוֹדֵעַ סְתָרֵינוּ — HE WATCHES AND KNOWS OUR SECRET THOUGHTS: 1
It is a huge change to come down from the Infinite to the individual, but far from being anticlimactic, the new perspective intensifies our perception of what God can mean in human life. Judah Halevi, the eleventh-century Spanish-Jewish poet, expressed this in his poem, "Lord, Where Shall I Find You?": "You are found in man's innermost heart, yet You fixed earth's boundaries." God, who is "enthroned among the cherubim," is part of each one of us: "He knows our secret thoughts."

גּוֹמֵל לְאִישׁ חֶסֶד כְּמִפְעָלוֹ — HE REWARDS THE GOOD DEEDS OF MEN: The 2
problem of good and evil is central to religious faith. One accepts in this principle that Providence ultimately blesses those who lead a moral life.

יִשְׁלַח . . . מְשִׁיחֵנוּ — HE WILL SEND OUR MESSIAH: In the Ani Ma'amin, this 3
twelfth principle has a touch of irony: "I believe with perfect faith in the coming of the Messiah; and even though he tarry, I will wait for him daily."

מְשִׁיחֵנוּ — OUR MESSIAH: In his Guide to the Perplexed, Maimonides tried to soften 4
the expectation of a supernatural savior, writing, instead, of a Messiah who will be an earthly king, a descendent of David. The Messiah will restore the Jews to their ancient land, bringing peace to the world.

מֵתִים יְחַיֶּה — HE RENEWS LIFE BEYOND DEATH: In Hebrew, the words mean 5
literally: "God will revive the dead." Maimonides' writings make it clear that he could not really accept the idea of physical resurrection, which was widespread among Jews in his time. It is the spirit in men and women that is immortal.

סֵדֶר מִנְהָגִים

AN
ORDER OF
RITUAL

הַדְלָקַת הַנֵּרוֹת

אַב הָרַחֲמִים, אָנָּא מְשֹׁךְ חַסְדְּךָ
עָלַי וְעַל קְרוֹבַי הָאֲהוּבִים,
וְשִׂים שָׁלוֹם אוֹרָה וְשִׂמְחָה
בִּמְעוֹנֵנוּ, כִּי עִמְּךָ מְקוֹר חַיִּים,
בְּאוֹרְךָ נִרְאֶה אוֹר. אָמֵן.

1

2

Father of mercy, bestow Your lovingkindness on me and my loved ones, near and dear to me. May peace and light and joy abide forever in our home, for with You is the fountain of life; in Your light, we see light. Amen.

The blessing is said
after the Shabbat lights are kindled:

בָּרוּךְ אַתָּה יְיָ,
אֱלֹהֵינוּ מֶלֶךְ הָעוֹלָם,
אֲשֶׁר קִדְּשָׁנוּ בְּמִצְוֹתָיו
וְצִוָּנוּ לְהַדְלִיק נֵר שֶׁל שַׁבָּת.

3

4,5

Blessed is the Lord our God, King of the Universe,
who hallows us with His mitzvot, and has commanded us to kindle the Sabbath light.

1 אַב הָרַחֲמִים — FATHER OF MERCY: This meditation is taken from the prayerbook edited by S. Singer in London in 1908.

2 מְקוֹר חַיִּים — FOUNTAIN OF LIFE: Shabbat is much more than a day of rest from work. The words we recite from the Bible are: "And God blessed the seventh day *and sanctified it.*" We feel the holiness of Shabbat in the mood it generates—the joy of worship, the love of family and friends. Life is not passive on Shabbat but intense in feeling. It is a day in which the purpose of life can be expressed in us.

3 קִדְּשָׁנוּ בְּמִצְוֹתָיו — HALLOWS US WITH HIS MITZVOT: *Mitzvot* is usually translated as "commandments," which can sound stern and forbidding. But a *mitzvah* in Jewish life is an act of love and devotion. It is a *mitzvah* to be kind and charitable. It is a *mitzvah* to be honest and truthful. It is a *mitzvah* to follow the rituals of Jewish life that have given us the concept of holiness. This is why the simple act of kindling the Shabbat lights is a *mitzvah,* and very dear to us.

4 לְהַדְלִיק — TO KINDLE: The Talmud tells us that as far back as Temple times a *shofar* was sounded when dusk was falling, as a signal to the citizens "to kindle the Sabbath lamp." In our minds, we still hear this trumpet sound, a salute to the magic of Shabbat.

5 לְהַדְלִיק נֵר שֶׁל שַׁבָּת — TO KINDLE THE SABBATH LIGHT: In itself, the Shabbat light offers only a small flicker, but "how far that little candle throws its beams." In the glow of our ceremony, at home and in synagogue, we are aware of myriad candles glowing at this very moment all over the world, celebrating the holiness of life and the aspiration of the Jewish people.

בִּרְכַּת הַבָּנִים

For a son:		
יְשִׂמְךָ אֱלֹהִים כְּאֶפְרַיִם וְכִמְנַשֶּׁה.	1	May God make you as Ephraim and Manasseh.
For a daughter:		
יְשִׂמֵךְ אֱלֹהִים כְּשָׂרָה, רִבְקָה, רָחֵל, וְלֵאָה.	2	May God make you as Sarah, Rebekkah, Rachel, and Leah.
For all children:		
יְבָרֶכְךָ יְיָ וְיִשְׁמְרֶךָ. יָאֵר יְיָ פָּנָיו אֵלֶיךָ וִיחֻנֶּךָ. יִשָּׂא יְיָ פָּנָיו אֵלֶיךָ וְיָשֵׂם לְךָ שָׁלוֹם.	3	May the Lord bless you and keep you. May the Lord let His presence shine on you and be gracious to you. May He shed His radiance around you and grant you peace.

BLESSING THE CHILDREN: In keeping with Shabbat as a family celebration, it is an old tradition that father blesses the children before sitting down to the Shabbat meal. Today, it would be natural for father and mother to do this jointly.

כְּאֶפְרַיִם וְכִמְנַשֶּׁה — AS EPHRAIM AND MANASSEH: The source of this blessing 1 is the 48th chapter of Genesis. Joseph has brought his aged father Jacob to live in Egypt. Jacob is about to die. Joseph brings his two sons to be blessed by their grandfather. With great effect, the narrative now calls Jacob by the name given him by the angel: Israel. With the children on his knee, Israel puts his right hand (a sign of favor) on Ephraim, though he is the younger; and with hindsight we know that this is because Ephraim will have a key place in the distribution of territory in the Holy Land. Israel foretells the future of the two boys and then blesses them, saying: "In thee shall Israel bless, saying: God make you as Ephraim and Manasseh."

כְּשָׂרָה, רִבְקָה, רָחֵל, וְלֵאָה — AS SARAH, REBEKKAH, RACHEL AND LEAH: 2 These are, of course, the wives of the patriarchs, Abraham, Isaac, and Jacob. These women are always thought of as the mothers of the nation.

יְבָרֶכְךָ יְיָ וְיִשְׁמְרֶךָ — MAY GOD BLESS AND KEEP YOU: This is the blessing 3 given in the book of Numbers, verses 6:24–26 that Aaron the High Priest was told to use when he and his sons blessed the people Israel. It has become a cherished blessing in Jewish (and Christian) ceremony. Among traditional Jews, it is recited with particular effect in the synagogue on holy days by Jews recognized as being of priestly descent. In Jewish teaching, the priest may recite the words, but the blessing that flows is from God. This is explicit in the Bible verse which follows the blessing: "And they [the priests] shall put My Name on the children of Israel, and I will bless them."

In this happy folk song, we sing *Shalom*
to "the ministering angels" who—according to
Jewish legend—hover in the air around us.

SHALOM ALECHEM

שָׁלוֹם עֲלֵיכֶם

<table>
<tr>
<td>
1 שָׁלוֹם עֲלֵיכֶם מַלְאֲכֵי הַשָּׁרֵת
2 מַלְאֲכֵי עֶלְיוֹן,
מִמֶּלֶךְ מַלְכֵי הַמְּלָכִים
הַקָּדוֹשׁ בָּרוּךְ הוּא.

בּוֹאֲכֶם לְשָׁלוֹם מַלְאֲכֵי הַשָּׁלוֹם
מַלְאֲכֵי עֶלְיוֹן,
מִמֶּלֶךְ מַלְכֵי הַמְּלָכִים
הַקָּדוֹשׁ בָּרוּךְ הוּא.
</td>
<td>
Peace unto you, ministering angels,
Messengers of the Most High,
From the King, the King of Kings,
the Holy One, blessed be He.

Come in peace, messengers of
peace,
Messengers of the Most High,
From the King, the King of Kings,
the Holy One, blessed be He.
</td>
</tr>
</table>

Shalom aleichem mal'achei hasharet mal'achei elyon
mimelech malchei hamelachim hakadosh baruch hu.
Bo'achem leshalom mal'achei hashalom mal'achei elyon
mimelech malchei hamelachim hakadosh baruch hu.

1 מַלְאֲכֵי הַשָּׁרֵת — MINISTERING ANGELS: The Hebrew word for "angel" is *mal'ach*, which means "messenger." In the patriarchal stories about angels, they never appear as unearthly creatures but always as humans, though with special knowledge and powers. The angels who promised Abraham a child through Sarah and who later went on to Sodom and Gomorrah are introduced simply: "And [Abram] lifted up his eyes and lo, three men stood by him . . ." (Genesis 18:2). The tone is the same later in the narration of Jacob's strange encounter that presaged the Jewish future: "And Jacob was left alone; and there wrestled a man with him until the breaking of the day . . ." (Genesis 32:24). As dawn breaks, Jacob learns that he has wrestled "with God"—a man wrestling with his fate. At this stage in the Bible, an angel is both natural and supernatural.

2 מַלְאֲכֵי עֶלְיוֹן — MESSENGERS OF THE MOST HIGH: Angels become more unearthly later. When the prophet Micaiah is asked whether the king should go into battle, his reply describes a vision he has had: "I saw the Lord sitting on his throne, and all the host of heaven standing by him on his right hand and on his left hand" (I Kings 22:19). This reminds one of the visions in Isaiah 6:1-3: "I saw the Lord sitting on a throne, high and lifted up, and his train filled the Temple. Above Him stood the Seraphim . . . crying out to one another; "Holy, holy, holy is the Lord of Hosts."

It was in the Babylonian Exile (sixth-fifth centuries B.C.E.) that the Jews began to embellish their own angel myths with more elaborate concepts. The Babylonians envisaged throngs of obedient gods or "angels" serving the superior gods in the heavenly courts and also moving among men. In time, the Jews adopted some of these ideas, though always within the bounds of their strict monotheism. Angels became fertile subjects for poetry and imagination. Sometimes they were depicted in wild visions, as in the book of Ezekiel. More often they surfaced in the quiet anecdotes of storytellers and preachers.

בָּרְכוּנִי לְשָׁלוֹם מַלְאֲכֵי הַשָּׁלוֹם מַלְאֲכֵי עֶלְיוֹן, מִמֶּלֶךְ מַלְכֵי הַמְּלָכִים הַקָּדוֹשׁ בָּרוּךְ הוּא. |1| Bless me with peace, messengers of peace, Messengers of the Most High, From the King, the King of Kings, the Holy One, blessed be He.
צֵאתְכֶם לְשָׁלוֹם מַלְאֲכֵי הַשָּׁלוֹם מַלְאֲכֵי עֶלְיוֹן, מִמֶּלֶךְ מַלְכֵי הַמְּלָכִים הַקָּדוֹשׁ בָּרוּךְ הוּא. |2 3 4| Depart in peace, messengers of peace, Messengers of the Most High, From the King, the King of Kings, the Holy One, blessed be He.

Barechuni leshalom mal'achei hashalom mal'achei elyon
mimelech malchei hamelachim hakadosh baruch hu.

Tzetchem leshalom mal'achei hashalom mal'achei elyon
mimelech malchei hamelachim hakadosh baruch hu.

בָּרְכוּנִי לְשָׁלוֹם — BLESS ME WITH PEACE: As symbols, the angels became familiar beings, giving body to the human experience of miracles and disasters, suffering and hope. The most somber of these beings was the Angel of Death; but even he, with his fateful message, might engage in conversation and put off the evil day by interceding with God, if good cause was shown. **1**

צֵאתְכֶם לְשָׁלוֹם — DEPART IN PEACE: According to the Talmud, every Jew is accompanied by two angels on his way home from synagogue on the Shabbat Eve. Some say that one of the angels is good and one wicked, illustrating the conflicting pull in our nature. However, in the *Shalom Aleichem* folk song we greet them all cheerfully, grateful for their protection. The air is full of wonder on Shabbat Eve, and this is what we are really singing about. **2**

מַלְאֲכֵי עֶלְיוֹן — MESSENGERS OF THE MOST HIGH: This is in line with the picture evoked in by the Psalmist, in which the angels execute God's will: "Bless the Lord, ye His angels that excel in strength, that do His commandments, hearkening unto the sound of His word. Bless ye the Lord, all ye His hosts; ye ministers that do His will" (Psalm 103:20–21). **3**

הַקָּדוֹשׁ בָּרוּךְ הוּא — THE HOLY ONE, BLESSED BE HE: The prophet Zechariah fills his book with stories of angels who stimulate his visions. An angel who talks to him intercedes with God, who sends a message of comfort and hope to Israel: "Thus saith the Lord: I have returned to Jerusalem with mercies; my house shall be built in it, and a line shall be stretched forth over Jerusalem. . . . The Lord shall comfort Zion, and shall yet choose Jerusalem" (Zechariah 1: 16–17). Daniel takes the visions further, showing angels with initiatives of their own to help mankind. In the book of Daniel we see them with names—Gabriel, Michael—and with power to act as guardians of individual peoples. Michael is the champion of Israel. **4**

אֵשֶׁת חַיִל

The husband says to his wife:

Proverbs 31:10-31

אֵשֶׁת חַיִל מִי יִמְצָא,
וְרָחֹק מִפְּנִינִים מִכְרָהּ.
בָּטַח בָּהּ לֵב בַּעְלָהּ,
וְשָׁלָל לֹא יֶחְסָר.

[1,2]

[3]

What a joy is a valiant woman!
Her worth is beyond rubies.
The heart of her husband trusts in
her; nothing they need is
lacking.

BLESSINGS BETWEEN HUSBAND AND WIFE: By old tradition, the husband returning home from synagogue on Shabbat Eve is so moved by the thought of how his wife has kept the home going all week and is now going to produce a marvelous Shabbat meal that he recites in her honor a long passage from the book of Proverbs (Proverbs 31:10–31) that sings the praises of valiant homemakers.

Today, in the spirit of our time, this seems too one-sided. Certainly, the husband shall be free to say lovely things about his wife; but why should not the wife, at the same time, say lovely things about her husband? As always, there is a passage in the Bible ready for this: the first Psalm.

Both passages are equally lyrical, and both create a very individual picture. It is clear that the author of the passage in Proverbs has no timid anonymous housewife in mind. The woman he describes—his own wife?—bears the great responsibilities of growing, weaving, buying, and selling which she carries out on a big scale and with total authority; but at the same time, she is handsome, beautifully dressed, and has a good sense of humor.

On the other side, the passage we are proposing for the wife to recite is equally individual in style. Her husband is prosperous—"everything he does is successful"— but this is not why she loves him. It is his character, which comes out equally in his private and public lives. He is quiet, solid, totally reliable. He reads a lot, he studies the Torah, but there is nothing dry-as-dust about him. When one is with him, one feels the fertility of his mind: "He is like a tree planted beside pools of water . . . and its leaf never whithers."

[1] מִי יִמְצָא — WHAT A JOY: A literal translation of the Hebrew would be "Who shall find a valiant woman?" Apart from sounding skeptical, this misses the force of the Hebrew, which is expressing the delight of finding one.

[2] אֵשֶׁת חַיִל — VALIANT WOMAN: The conventional translation is "a woman of worth." The New English Bible makes it even duller with "a capable woman," which is extremely feeble for the amazing range of qualities in this lady. Besides, ḥayil means "strong," with special reference to the valor of soldiers. In Hebrew today, the same root is used for "soldier" (ḥayyal). This woman is not "capable" but "valiant," soldiering on day after day.

[3] וְשָׁלָל לֹא יֶחְסָר — NOTHING . . . IS LACKING: Literally: "gain" is not lacking.

93

גְּמָלַתְהוּ טוֹב וְלֹא רָע
כֹּל יְמֵי חַיֶּיהָ.
דָּרְשָׁה צֶמֶר וּפִשְׁתִּים,
וַתַּעַשׂ בְּחֵפֶץ כַּפֶּיהָ.
הָיְתָה כָּאֳנִיּוֹת סוֹחֵר 1
מִמֶּרְחָק תָּבִיא לַחְמָהּ.
וַתָּקָם בְּעוֹד לַיְלָה,
וַתִּתֵּן טֶרֶף לְבֵיתָהּ
וְחֹק לְנַעֲרֹתֶיהָ.
זָמְמָה שָׂדֶה וַתִּקָּחֵהוּ,
מִפְּרִי כַפֶּיהָ נָטְעָה כָּרֶם.
חָגְרָה בְעוֹז מָתְנֶיהָ,
וַתְּאַמֵּץ זְרוֹעֹתֶיהָ.
טָעֲמָה כִּי־טוֹב סַחְרָהּ,
לֹא יִכְבֶּה בַלַּיְלָה נֵרָהּ.
יָדֶיהָ שִׁלְּחָה בַכִּישׁוֹר,
וְכַפֶּיהָ תָּמְכוּ פָלֶךְ.
כַּפָּהּ פָּרְשָׂה לֶעָנִי,
וְיָדֶיהָ שִׁלְּחָה לָאֶבְיוֹן.
לֹא תִירָא לְבֵיתָהּ מִשָּׁלֶג,
כִּי כָל־בֵּיתָהּ לָבֻשׁ שָׁנִים. 2
מַרְבַדִּים עָשְׂתָה־לָּהּ,
שֵׁשׁ וְאַרְגָּמָן לְבוּשָׁהּ.

She does him good and not evil
all the days of her life.
She chooses wool and flax,
and toils at her work.
She is like the merchant ships:
she brings food from afar.
She rises while it is still night,
and sets out food for her
household and a portion for her
maidens.
She considers a field and buys it;
with her own earnings, she
plants a vineyard.
She sets about her duties with
vigor, and braces herself for the
work. She sees that her
business goes well; she never
puts out her lamp at night.
She takes the distaff in her hand,
and her fingers grasp the
spindle.
She is open-handed to the poor,
and is generous to the needy.
She has no fear for her
household when it snows, for
they are all clothed in scarlet
wool.
She makes her own coverings,
and clothing of fine linen and
purple.

כָּאֳנִיּוֹת סוֹחֵר — LIKE THE MERCHANT SHIPS: This is a very satisfying image, 1
conveying both the practical aspect of the ships, which, like the wife, carry home
everything the house needs, and also the grace and beauty with which the ships
move through dangerous waters to come safely home at last.

לָבֻשׁ שָׁנִים — CLOTHED IN SCARLET WOOL: Wool garments were garments of 2
very high quality and kept the wearer very warm. In poetry, "scarlet" stands out
very effectively in contrast to the whiteness of the snow in the previous line.

נוֹדָע בַּשְּׁעָרִים בַּעְלָהּ	1	Her husband is well known in the city gate, when he sits with the elders of the land.
בְּשִׁבְתּוֹ עִם זִקְנֵי־אָרֶץ.		
סָדִין עָשְׂתָה וַתִּמְכֹּר,		She makes fine linen and sells it, and supplies sashes to the merchant.
וַחֲגוֹר נָתְנָה לַכְּנַעֲנִי.		
עֹז וְהָדָר לְבוּשָׁהּ,		Strength and honor are her clothing; she is cheerful, never worried or morbid.
וַתִּשְׂחַק לְיוֹם אַחֲרוֹן.	2	
פִּיהָ פָּתְחָה בְחָכְמָה,		When she talks, it is with wisdom; words of kindness are on her tongue.
וְתוֹרַת חֶסֶד עַל לְשׁוֹנָהּ.		
צוֹפִיָּה הֲלִיכוֹת בֵּיתָהּ,		She keeps her eye on the doings of her household, and does not eat the bread of idleness.
וְלֶחֶם עַצְלוּת לֹא תֹאכֵל.		
קָמוּ בָנֶיהָ וַיְאַשְּׁרוּהָ,		Her children with one accord call her happy; her husband, too, sings her praises.
בַּעְלָהּ וַיְהַלְלָהּ.		
רַבּוֹת בָּנוֹת עָשׂוּ חָיִל,		Many a woman does well, but you excel over them all.
וְאַתְּ עָלִית עַל כֻּלָּנָה.		
שֶׁקֶר הַחֵן וְהֶבֶל הַיֹּפִי,		Charm can be false, beauty fleeting; it is a God-fearing woman who is honored.
אִשָּׁה יִרְאַת יְיָ הִיא תִתְהַלָּל.	3	
תְּנוּ־לָהּ מִפְּרִי יָדֶיהָ,		Sing her praises for the work of her hands; let her own deeds praise her in the city gates.
וִיהַלְלוּהָ בַשְּׁעָרִים מַעֲשֶׂיהָ.	4	

---

1 בַּשְּׁעָרִים — IN THE CITY GATE: The gate is the meeting place for political and social talk among the men. It is absolutely in character for this woman to have a husband who is important in his own right, and of whom she is proud.

2 וַתִּשְׂחַק לְיוֹם אַחֲרוֹן — IS CHEERFUL: The Hebrew means literally "She laughs about 'the last day',"—making light of death. The sentence attributes to her a marvelous self-confidence, a sense of humor. Nothing gets her down.

3 אִשָּׁה יִרְאַת יְיָ — GOD-FEARING WOMAN: Behind her good humor and resourcefulness, she is serious, and that is what her husband likes particularly.

4 בַּשְּׁעָרִים — IN THE CITY GATES: We have already heard that her husband spends much of his time at the city gate. Perhaps, in the midst of his discussions of public matters, he feels slightly guilty about meeting to talk, when he thinks of all that his wife does on her own. Her husband is certainly proud of her, and presumably is always talking about her, indeed boasting about her.

WIFE'S DECLARATION

אַשְׁרֵי הָאִישׁ

The wife may respond:

Psalm 1

1 אַשְׁרֵי הָאִישׁ אֲשֶׁר לֹא הָלַךְ
בַּעֲצַת רְשָׁעִים,
וּבְדֶרֶךְ חַטָּאִים לֹא עָמָד,
2 וּבְמוֹשַׁב לֵצִים לֹא יָשָׁב.
3 כִּי אִם בְּתוֹרַת יְיָ חֶפְצוֹ,
וּבְתוֹרָתוֹ יֶהְגֶּה יוֹמָם וָלָיְלָה.
4 וְהָיָה כְּעֵץ שָׁתוּל עַל פַּלְגֵי־מָיִם,
אֲשֶׁר פִּרְיוֹ יִתֵּן בְּעִתּוֹ
וְעָלֵהוּ לֹא יִבּוֹל
וְכֹל אֲשֶׁר יַעֲשֶׂה יַצְלִיחַ.
לֹא־כֵן הָרְשָׁעִים כִּי אִם כַּמֹּץ
אֲשֶׁר תִּדְּפֶנּוּ רוּחַ.
עַל־כֵּן לֹא יָקֻמוּ רְשָׁעִים בַּמִּשְׁפָּט
וְחַטָּאִים בַּעֲדַת צַדִּיקִים.
כִּי יוֹדֵעַ יְיָ דֶּרֶךְ צַדִּיקִים
וְדֶרֶךְ רְשָׁעִים תֹּאבֵד.

Happy is the man who walks not by
the counsel of the wicked, and
stands not on the path of
sinners, and sits not in the seat
of the scoffers.
But his delight is in the Lord's
teaching, and he meditates on
the Lord's teaching day and
night.
He is like a tree planted beside pools
of water, which yields its fruit
in season, and whose leaf never
withers; in whatever he does he
shall prosper.
The wicked are not like this, but are
chaff driven by the wind.
The wicked do not stand up in
judgment, they are not in the
assembly of the righteous.
The way of the righteous is to the
Lord; the way of the wicked
leads to doom.

אַשְׁרֵי הָאִישׁ — HAPPY IS THE MAN: This is a psalm of quiet reflection, contrast-
ing two ways of life: living with evil people, and living with decent people. The late
Mitchell Dahood, the Jesuit scholar, said: "This psalm is more than an introduction
to the Psalter; it is rather a précis of the Book of Psalms." [1]

וּבְמוֹשַׁב לֵצִים — IN THE SEAT OF THE SCOFFERS: Scoffers are always treated
in the Wisdom literature of the Bible as a specially pernicious kind of evil-doers.
They don't just break God's law: they pour scorn on all who take moral conduct
seriously. One is reminded of the passage: "Cast out the scoffer, and discord will
leave with him; disputes and name-calling will cease" (Proverbs 22:10). [2]

בְּתוֹרַת יְיָ — IN THE LORD'S TEACHING: Literally: "the Torah of the Lord,"
using Torah in its general sense to represent God's law and teaching. [3]

כְּעֵץ שָׁתוּל עַל־פַּלְגֵי־מָיִם — LIKE A TREE PLANTED BESIDE POOLS OF WATER:
This beautiful analogy appears in more graphic detail in the book of Jeremiah. The
man "whose heart has departed from God" is like a desert bush "in a desert where
no man can live," while a man trusting in God "is like a tree planted by the
waterside, that stretches its roots by the stream" (Jeremiah 17:5–8). [4]

The blessing on wine is preceded by the
passage in Genesis that describes the origin
of the day of rest in relation to Creation.
(Genesis 1:31–2:3).

KIDDUSH

קִדּוּשׁ

Genesis 1:31–2:3

וַיְהִי־עֶרֶב וַיְהִי־בֹקֶר יוֹם הַשִּׁשִּׁי.
וַיְכֻלּוּ הַשָּׁמַיִם וְהָאָרֶץ
וְכָל־צְבָאָם.
וַיְכַל אֱלֹהִים בַּיּוֹם הַשְּׁבִיעִי
מְלַאכְתּוֹ אֲשֶׁר עָשָׂה,
וַיִּשְׁבֹּת בַּיּוֹם הַשְּׁבִיעִי
מִכָּל־מְלַאכְתּוֹ אֲשֶׁר עָשָׂה.
וַיְבָרֶךְ אֱלֹהִים אֶת־יוֹם הַשְּׁבִיעִי
וַיְקַדֵּשׁ אֹתוֹ,
כִּי בוֹ שָׁבַת מִכָּל־מְלַאכְתּוֹ
אֲשֶׁר בָּרָא אֱלֹהִים לַעֲשׂוֹת.

1

Evening came and morning came —
the sixth day.
Thus heaven and earth were
complete, with all their throng.
On the seventh day, God had
completed His work. He rested
on the seventh day from all the
work He had done.
And God blessed the seventh day
and sanctified it; for on that day
He rested from all the work
which He had created and done.

1   וַיְכֻלּוּ הַשָּׁמַיִם וְהָאָרֶץ — THUS HEAVEN AND EARTH WERE COMPLETE: This
powerful summary of Creation carries great significance for Jews, as Professor
E. A. Speiser pointed out in his commentary on Genesis in the Anchor Bible:

We are given the barest statement of a sequence of facts, resulting
from the fiat of the supreme and absolute master of the universe. Yet
the account has a grandeur and a dramatic impact of its own.

The stark simplicity of this passage is by no means a mark of meagre
writing ability. It is the result of a special cultivation, a process in
which each detail was refined through endless probing and each word
subjected to the most minute scrutiny. The objective was to set forth,
in a manner that must not presume in any way to edit the achievement
of the Creator, not a theory but a credo, a credo untinged by the least
hint of speculation.

The point here is not whether this account of Creation conforms to
the scientific data of today but what it meant to, and how it was
arrived at, by the writer concerned.

It is clear, Speiser argues, that the account of Creation in Genesis was linked to the
current Mesopotamian ideas, and this is natural; Mesopotamian science was
"highly advanced, respected and influential." But the Hebrews put their own mark
on what lay around them:

The Babylonian creation story features a succession of various rival
deities. The Biblical version, on the other hand, is determined by the
monotheistic conception in the absolute sense of the term.

Raising the kiddush cup,
the reader invites attention:

סַבְרֵי מָרָנָן וְרַבּוֹתַי.

בָּרוּךְ אַתָּה יְיָ
אֱלֹהֵינוּ מֶלֶךְ הָעוֹלָם,
בּוֹרֵא פְּרִי הַגָּפֶן.

בָּרוּךְ אַתָּה יְיָ
אֱלֹהֵינוּ מֶלֶךְ הָעוֹלָם,
אֲשֶׁר קִדְּשָׁנוּ בְּמִצְוֹתָיו וְרָצָה בָנוּ,
וְשַׁבַּת קָדְשׁוֹ בְּאַהֲבָה וּבְרָצוֹן
הִנְחִילָנוּ, זִכָּרוֹן לְמַעֲשֵׂה
בְרֵאשִׁית.
כִּי הוּא יוֹם תְּחִלָּה לְמִקְרָאֵי
קֹדֶשׁ, זֵכֶר לִיצִיאַת מִצְרָיִם.
כִּי בָנוּ בָחַרְתָּ וְאוֹתָנוּ קִדַּשְׁתָּ
מִכָּל־הָעַמִּים, וְשַׁבַּת קָדְשְׁךָ
בְּאַהֲבָה וּבְרָצוֹן הִנְחַלְתָּנוּ.
בָּרוּךְ אַתָּה יְיָ, מְקַדֵּשׁ הַשַּׁבָּת.

Be blessed O Lord our God,
   King of the universe,
   who created the fruit of the
   vine.
Be blessed O Lord our God,
   King of the universe,
Who sanctified us with His *mitzvot*
   and has shown favor to us:
With love and favor He has given us
   His holy Sabbath as a memory
   of Creation.
That day is the first of our holy
   convocations, in memory of the
   Exodus from Egypt.
You have chosen us and sanctified
   us among all peoples, and with
   love and favor You have given
   us the heritage of Your holy
   Sabbath.
Be blessed, O Lord, who has
   sanctified the Sabbath.

תְּחִלָּה לְמִקְרָאֵי קֹדֶשׁ — THE FIRST OF OUR HOLY CONVOCATIONS: The priority of Shabbat is attested to by its place in the Ten Commandments; and this is reinforced by the prophets. Jeremiah reports a vision (Jeremiah 17:19-27) in which God tells him that the people must be warned against doing any kind of work on Shabbat. Ezekiel (chapter 20) echoes this. Nehemiah reports the public confession in which Shabbat is hailed as the most important of the laws, for it was the breach of Shabbat that had led to exile (13:15-22). [1]

בְּאַהֲבָה וּבְרָצוֹן — WITH LOVE AND FAVOR: Once again, the word *ratzon* (favor or pleasure) is brought into the Shabbat celebration. It embraces the idea of *imitatio dei*: God has pleasure in Shabbat, and the people of Israel have a parallel pleasure in everything that flows from Shabbat. [2]

הִנְחַלְתָּנוּ — YOU HAVE GIVEN US THE HERITAGE: One is reminded of the words of Solomon Schechter: "Jews do not keep the Sabbath so much because it is in the Bible but because of the emphasis the Biblical injunctions concerning the Sabbath receive in the history of Jewish life, thought and experience." [3]

נְטִילַת יָדַיִם

בָּרוּךְ אַתָּה יְיָ
אֱלֹהֵינוּ מֶלֶךְ הָעוֹלָם,
אֲשֶׁר קִדְּשָׁנוּ בְּמִצְוֹתָיו
וְצִוָּנוּ עַל נְטִילַת יָדָיִם.

1

Blessed be the Lord our God,
King of the Universe,
who sanctified us with His *mitzvot*,
and commanded us on the
washing of hands.

1 עַל נְטִילַת יָדִים — WASHING OF HANDS: The universal practice among Jews of washing the hands before breaking bread for a meal combines two themes—ritual purity and personal hygiene.

Ritual purity is treated at great length in the Torah and the Talmud. The basic idea is that the human body is something designed by God and must therefore be treated with respect, and made ritually clean, in a ceremonial ablution of "impurities" that run counter to the natural healthy state. One must be made "clean" through the rituals in order to go on living normally and also to take part in a religious service.

In the Bible, the central figure who returns to ritual purity is the priest. In this role, he himself has to guard against impurity. Among many prohibitions is one which states that he cannot serve if he has a "blemish" (a long list of these physical abnormalities is given in Leviticus 21: 18–21); and before he approaches the altar, he must wash hands and feet in the laver of the courtyard (Exodus 30:18–21). He is then free to take part in the enormously detailed rituals through which an "unclean" person gets rid of impurity, as set out basically in Leviticus, chapters 11–17, and Numbers, chapter 19. Washing plays a large role in these rituals; and there were sects among the Jews who gave this extreme significance, like the Dead Sea Scroll sect, or the Baptists.

Inevitably, hygiene overlaps with the theme of ritual purity. Biblical provisions on "unclean" food are stated in religious terms, and the same is true of the rabbinical emphasis on personal hygiene. Much washing of the hands is laid down by the rabbis, together with many rules on cleanliness generally, such as on the handling of food, and keeping the home, the markets and the streets clean. It is thought that the lower death rate for Jews during the Black Death of the 14th century must be attributed to this.

But if the Jewish precepts on personal cleanliness are hygienic, the motivation for observance is not health but the observance of precepts as laid down in the Torah. The same is true of the numerous regulations on what a Jew may eat. It is often argued that the prohibitions guarded Jews against unhealthy food, and this may be true. But that is not why the dietary laws were observed. They were not to make Jews *healthy* but to make them *holy*. Obedience to the Torah served to provide Jews with a set of principles by which to live.

הַמּוֹצִיא

בָּרוּךְ אַתָּה יְיָ
אֱלֹהֵינוּ מֶלֶךְ הָעוֹלָם,
הַמּוֹצִיא לֶחֶם מִן הָאָרֶץ.

Blessed be God, our Lord,
King of the Universe,
who brings bread from the earth.

1

HAMOTZI: The blessing on bread starts the meal in a ritualized form. Bread was always basic; one "breaks bread" in starting a meal. When one has made the blessing on bread, the rabbis ruled that no other food blessing need be recited except on wine and fruit.

The form of *hamotzi* is very old. The Mishnah (the code edited in the 2nd century C.E.) reports it (*Berachot* 6:1). The blessing covers even unleavened bread; for at the Passover *seder*, when we eat *matzah*, we first recite the ordinary *hamotzi*, and then the special blessing for *matzah*, unleavened bread.

In the cult of the ancient Hebrews, the relationship to God was actualized by bringing sacrifices to Him of food in various forms, animal and vegetable, that were important in the life of the worshiper, and were thus to be "shared" with God and blessed by him as a good omen for future fertility. Prominent among the sacrifices were animals and fowl, with rituals for their slaughter, cooking and consumption carefully defined. But grain offerings were also very important.

The word *minhah*, which means a gift, is used generally in the Bible for an offering, but came to be applied specially to grain offerings, prepared as food. The various ways in which the offerings were prepared are described in the second chapter of the book of Leviticus. The worshiper could offer flour mixed with oil, ready for cooking, or loaves or cakes baked on a grill or in an oven. Every grain offering, in whatever form, had to contain a little salt, and if baked it was to be unleavened, at any time of the year. As we all know that the Shabbat loaf today is called a *hallah*, it is interesting to find this and another word used in the Bible for two kinds of unleavened bread baked in an oven and brought as sacrifices. If the flour is mixed with oil, they are called *hallot matzot* ("unleavened hallahs"); if the cakes are smeared with oil, they are called *rekikei matzot* ("unleavened wafers").

It is traditional for the Shabbat table to have two hallahs, in memory of the fact that when the manna was collected by the Israelites in the wilderness, they found a double portion on Fridays, to save them from the labor of collecting it on Shabbat (Exodus 16:5).

On Shabbat and holy days, this happy Psalm is
sung by all the company before the recital
of *Birkat Hamazon* (Grace after the Meal). This has
made Psalm 126 one of the best-known
and best-loved psalms by Jews.

A PSALM BEFORE BIRKAT HAMAZON

שִׁיר הַמַּעֲלוֹת

Psalm 126

שִׁיר הַמַּעֲלוֹת
בְּשׁוּב יְיָ אֶת־שִׁיבַת צִיּוֹן
הָיִינוּ כְּחֹלְמִים.
אָז יִמָּלֵא שְׂחוֹק פִּינוּ
וּלְשׁוֹנֵנוּ רִנָּה.
אָז יֹאמְרוּ בַגּוֹיִם
הִגְדִּיל יְיָ לַעֲשׂוֹת עִם אֵלֶּה.
הִגְדִּיל יְיָ לַעֲשׂוֹת עִמָּנוּ
הָיִינוּ שְׂמֵחִים.
שׁוּבָה יְיָ אֶת־שְׁבִיתֵנוּ
כַּאֲפִיקִים בַּנֶּגֶב.
הַזֹּרְעִים בְּדִמְעָה בְּרִנָּה יִקְצֹרוּ.
הָלוֹךְ יֵלֵךְ וּבָכֹה
נֹשֵׂא מֶשֶׁךְ הַזָּרַע,
בֹּא יָבֹא בְרִנָּה נֹשֵׂא אֲלֻמֹּתָיו.

1
2
3
4

(A processional song.)
When the Lord turned again the
captivity of Zion, we were like
them that dream.
Then was our mouth filled with
laughter and our tongue with
singing; then said they among
the nations: the Lord has done
great things for them.
Great things indeed the Lord did for
us, whereof we are glad.
Turn around our captivity, O Lord,
like streams in the Negev.
They that sow in tears shall reap in
joy.
He who goes forth weeping,
carrying a bag of seed, shall
come back rejoicing, carrying
his sheaves.

1 שִׁיר הַמַּעֲלוֹת — A PROCESSIONAL SONG: Fifteen psalms have this title, *shir
hama'alot*, which is, literally, "a song of steps." There may have been a staircase in
the Temple to which there was a procession, but scholars are uncertain.

2 שׁוּבָה יְיָ אֶת־שְׁבִיתֵנוּ — TURN AROUND OUR CAPTIVITY, O LORD: The Hebrew
words contain a pun that is untranslatable. The intent is clearly to call for a reverse,
just as a dry *wadi* ("riverbed") in the Negev is suddenly flooded with water in a
rainstorm.

3 הָלוֹךְ יֵלֵךְ — HE WHO GOES FORTH: In Hebrew, the construction is marvelously
effective. The words mean literally: "walking, walking and weeping." This "double"
construction is echoed in the parallel phrase, which might be translated: "turning,
returning in joy" (or with a shout of joy).

4 נֹשֵׂא מֶשֶׁךְ הַזָּרַע — CARRYING A BAG OF SEED: The Hebrew word *meshech*
is somewhat obscure, but the intent of the verse is clear. The sentence on which is
depends would be translated literally: "They who sow in sadness, in joy shall reap."

101

With the meal ending, the diners look around
the table in genial mood, to see if all are
ready for the relaxed, happy recital
of prayers—sometimes in song—that will
constitute the Grace.

INVITATION TO BIRKAT HAMAZON

בִּרְכַּת הַזִּמּוּן

The host begins:

רַבּוֹתַי נְבָרֵךְ. | 1

Friends, shall we say the blessing on the meal?

Company, then host:

יְהִי שֵׁם יְיָ מְבֹרָךְ
מֵעַתָּה וְעַד עוֹלָם. | 2

May the name of the Lord be blessed from this time forth and forever.

Host:

בִּרְשׁוּת מָרָנָן וְרַבּוֹתַי
נְבָרֵךְ (אֱלֹהֵינוּ) שֶׁאָכַלְנוּ מִשֶּׁלּוֹ.

If it please you, let us bless our God from whose bounty we have eaten.

Company, then host:

בָּרוּךְ (אֱלֹהֵינוּ) שֶׁאָכַלְנוּ מִשֶּׁלּוֹ
וּבְטוּבוֹ חָיִינוּ. | 3,4

Blessed is our God from whose bounty we have eaten and through whose goodness we live.

All

בָּרוּךְ הוּא וּבָרוּךְ שְׁמוֹ.

Blessed is He, and blessed is His Name.

נְבָרֵךְ — SHALL WE SAY THE BLESSING: The Rabbis laid it down (Mishnah *Berachot* 7:1) that if a minimum of three ate together, they should say a joint grace. The larger the number, the more elaborately the invitation to say Grace should be framed, with grandiloquent descriptions of God's bounty. The *mitzvah* of saying Grace is linked to the Bible verse: "Thou shalt eat and be satisfied and bless the Lord thy God for the good land which He has given you" (Deuteronomy 8:10). | 1

שֵׁם יְיָ — THE NAME OF THE LORD: The Grace picks up the mood from the meal itself, which has given the company a chance to discuss "words of Torah." There is a relevant saying by Rabbi Shimon (Ethics of the Fathers 3:4): "If three have eaten at a table and have spoken no words of Torah, it is as if they had eaten of sacrifices to dead idols, . . . but if three have eaten at a table and have spoken there words of Torah, it is as if they had eaten at the table of the Divine Presence." | 2

בָּרוּךְ אֱלֹהֵינוּ — BLESSED IS OUR GOD: The word *elohenu* (our God) is added when at least ten are present, constituting a *minyan* (an official quorum). | 3

שֶׁאָכַלְנוּ מִשֶּׁלּוֹ — FROM WHOSE BOUNTY WE HAVE EATEN: The Midrash tells us that Father Abraham, who won the hearts of strangers by his lavish hospitality, led them afterwards into a recital of the Grace, through which he taught them to believe in God, "from whose bounty" they had eaten. | 4

בִּרְכַּת הַמָּזוֹן

בָּרוּךְ אַתָּה יְיָ,
אֱלֹהֵינוּ מֶלֶךְ הָעוֹלָם,
הַזָּן אֶת־הָעוֹלָם כֻּלּוֹ בְּטוּבוֹ
בְּחֵן בְּחֶסֶד וּבְרַחֲמִים,
הוּא נוֹתֵן לֶחֶם לְכָל־בָּשָׂר,
כִּי לְעוֹלָם חַסְדּוֹ.
וּבְטוּבוֹ הַגָּדוֹל תָּמִיד לֹא חָסַר
לָנוּ וְאַל יֶחְסַר־לָנוּ מָזוֹן לְעוֹלָם
וָעֶד, בַּעֲבוּר שְׁמוֹ הַגָּדוֹל.
כִּי הוּא זָן וּמְפַרְנֵס לַכֹּל
וּמֵטִיב לַכֹּל וּמֵכִין מָזוֹן
לְכָל־בְּרִיּוֹתָיו אֲשֶׁר בָּרָא.
בָּרוּךְ אַתָּה יְיָ, הַזָּן אֶת־הַכֹּל.

1,2

3

4

Be blessed, O Lord our God, King of the universe, who feeds the whole world with His goodness, grace, lovingkindness and mercy;
He gives food to all mankind, for His kindness endures forever.
Because of His great goodness, food has never failed us; may it never fail us forever and ever, in fulfillment of His great Name.
He feeds and nourishes all, and does good to all, and provides food for all the creatures He has created.
Be blessed, O Lord, who feeds all.

1   הַזָּן — WHO FEEDS: In this, the first of the three basic themes of the Grace (*Birkat Hamazon*), we thank God for providing food for all His creatures. The other two themes we shall meet are God's provision of "the good land" of Israel, and the redemption He will bring to His people.

2   הָעוֹלָם כֻּלּוֹ — THE WHOLE WORLD: Like the *Tefillah*, the *Birkat Hamazon* opens with a universalistic view of God as creator and sustainer of all—the universe, the world we know, and mankind within this world.

3   תָּמִיד לֹא חָסַר לָנוּ — HAS NEVER FAILED US: According to the Babylonian Talmud (*Berachot* 48b), this first benediction was instituted by Moses when the manna fell from heaven. The drama of this episode (Exodus 16) is etched in Jewish folk memory. The Israelites, wandering in the wilderness, are "murmuring" against Moses for having taken them out of Egypt "where we sat by the meatpots and ate bread to the full." In the wilderness, they are starving. God says to Moses: "Behold, I will rain bread from heaven for you." This was the miracle of the manna. When they gathered it, no one had any lack: "they gathered, every man according to his eating." It is a good setting for the first theme of the Grace: God sustaining His creatures with food.

4   הוּא זָן וּמְפַרְנֵס לַכֹּל — HE FEEDS AND NOURISHES ALL: The universalism of this blessing is symbolized in a ruling of the rabbis in the Mishnah (*Sotah* 7:1) that the Grace is one of the prayers which may be recited in any language. By an old tradition, some bread should be left on the table until the Grace has been completed, in order to illustrate God's bounty, acknowledged in the Grace.

נוֹדֶה לְךָ יְיָ אֱלֹהֵינוּ כִּי הִנְחַלְתָּנוּ אֶרֶץ חֶמְדָּה טוֹבָה וּרְחָבָה, בְּרִית וְתוֹרָה, חַיִּים וּמָזוֹן, וְעַל כֻּלָּם אֲנוּ מוֹדִים לָךְ וּמְבָרְכִים אֶת־שְׁמְךָ לְעוֹלָם וָעֶד. בָּרוּךְ אַתָּה יְיָ, עַל הָאָרֶץ וְעַל הַמָּזוֹן.	We thank You, O Lord our God, that You gave us as a heritage a desirable, good and ample land, the Covenant and the Torah, life and food; For all of them we thank You and bless Your Name forever and ever. Be blessed, O Lord, for the land and for food.

נוֹדֶה לְךָ — WE THANK YOU: This paragraph, developing the second theme of the *Birkat Hamazon*—the land of Israel—is here in the shorter form presented in the *siddur* of the famous scholar Saadya Gaon (882-942). It has always been legitimate to use a shorter version of the Grace when circumstances make it hard to use a long one, as, for example, when a workman would not have time to recite the full prayer. But all can use a shorter version provided that the basic requirements are met, which are: that the first blessing on God's provision of food is retained, and that the two succeeding themes be clearly identified, the first dealing with the Land of Israel, the Covenant and the Torah, and the second with the hope of Redemption. Saadya's version, used here, clearly meets these basic requirements.

אֶרֶץ חֶמְדָּה טוֹבָה וּרְחָבָה — A DESIRABLE, GOOD AND AMPLE LAND: Something close to this phrase appears in the book of Exodus 3:8, when God says to Moses that He will bring the people of Israel out of Egypt "unto a good and ample land, a land flowing with milk and honey." It is remarkable how vivid was the concept of the beauty of the Holy Land to untold millions of Jews who could never hope to see it with their own eyes. Its physical beauty was evoked in the Psalms, which were recited constantly. It was with enormous joy that a Jew would recite, for example, Psalm 84: "How dear is Your dwelling-place, O Lord of Hosts; I pine, I faint for longing for the courts of the Lord." The most intense of all longings was "Next Year in Jerusalem." Judah Halevi (1085-1141) reflected these feelings in his many poems on Zion. In one of the most touching, he says how easily he could give up the comforts of life in the West for a chance to see the ruins of the Temple. His verse, with its puns and assonance, might be translated:

How light in my eyes to leave the bounty of Spain!
How bright in my eyes the dust of the Shrine again.

בְּרִית וְתוֹרָה — THE COVENANT AND THE TORAH: The beauty of the land itself was never the full reason for Israel's involvement. The land expressed Israel's spiritual links to the covenant and the Torah. It was always the *holy* land.

רַחֵם יְיָ אֱלֹהֵינוּ עָלֵינוּ,
עַל יִשְׂרָאֵל עַמֶּךָ,
וְעַל יְרוּשָׁלַיִם עִירֶךָ,
וְעַל הֵיכָלֶךָ וְעַל מְעוֹנֶךָ,
וְעַל צִיּוֹן מִשְׁכַּן כְּבוֹדֶךָ,
וְעַל הַבַּיִת הַגָּדוֹל וְהַקָּדוֹשׁ
אֲשֶׁר נִקְרָא שִׁמְךָ עָלָיו,
וּמַלְכוּת בֵּית דָּוִד מְהֵרָה תַּחֲזִיר.

On Shabbat:

רְצֵה וְהַחֲלִיצֵנוּ יְיָ אֱלֹהֵינוּ
בְּכָל־מִצְוֹתֶיךָ, וּמִצְוַת יוֹם
הַשְּׁבִיעִי הַגָּדוֹל וְהַקָּדוֹשׁ הַזֶּה.
כִּי יוֹם גָּדוֹל וְקָדוֹשׁ הוּא מִלְּפָנֶיךָ
וְנִשְׁבָּת־בּוֹ כְּמִצְוַת רְצוֹנֶךָ.
כִּרְצוֹנְךָ הָנַח לָנוּ וְאַל יְהִי
צָרָה וְיָגוֹן בְּיוֹם מְנוּחָתֵנוּ.

Have mercy on us, O Lord our God:
on Your people Israel, on
Jerusalem Your city, on Your
Temple, Your dwelling place, on
Zion the seat of Your glory, and
on the great and holy House
that was called by Your Name.
Restore speedily, we pray, the rule
of the House of David.

Accept with favor and support us, O
Lord our God, with all Your
mitzvot, and especially the *mitzvah*
of this great and holy Seventh
Day.
We rest on this day, great and holy
to You, fulfilling the *mitzvah* of
your will.
By Your will, grant us rest, with no
trouble or grief on this, our day
of rest.

1   עַל יְרוּשָׁלַיִם עִירֶךָ — ON JERUSALEM YOUR CITY: The rebuilding of Jerusalem, symbolizing the redemption of the people of Israel, is the third theme of the *Birkat Hamazon,* ending with *uvneh yerushalayim* ("rebuild Jerusalem") on page 106. The glories of the Temple are recalled nostalgically here, as in the famed sentence of Psalm 84: "I had rather be a doorkeeper in the House of God than dwell in the tents of wickedness"—the same thought expressed by Judah Halevi in his poem.

2   וְעַל צִיּוֹן מִשְׁכַּן כְּבוֹדֶךָ — ON ZION THE SEAT OF YOUR GLORY: The emphasis on the restoration of Jerusalem is in accord with the ordinance of the rabbis, that one must never forget the destruction of Jerusalem, even during meals (Babylonian Talmud, *Bava Batra* 60b).

3   וּמַלְכוּת בֵּית דָּוִד — THE RULE OF THE HOUSE OF DAVID: This shorter version, from Saadya Gaon's *siddur,* is a prayer for the restoration of the rule of "the House of David," whereas the longer version in prayerbooks asks for the return of "the House of David Your Messiah ("anointed one"). There is a similar omission by Saadya of the term Messiah in the prayer recited on *Rosh Ḥodesh* (see page 106) and during festivals. Perhaps Saadya felt it wise not to talk too easily about the coming of the Messiah.

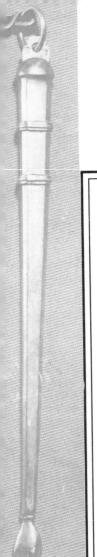

On Rosh Ḥodesh:

אֱלֹהֵינוּ וֵאלֹהֵי אֲבוֹתֵינוּ,
יַעֲלֶה וְיָבֹא, יַגִּיעַ וְיֵרָאֶה,
יֵרָצֶה וְיִפָּקֵד זִכְרוֹנֵנוּ
וְזִכְרוֹן אֲבוֹתֵינוּ,
וְזִכְרוֹן יְרוּשָׁלַיִם עִירֶךָ,
וְזִכְרוֹן עַמְּךָ כָּל־בֵּית יִשְׂרָאֵל
לְפָנֶיךָ לְטוֹבָה
בְּיוֹם רֹאשׁ הַחֹדֶשׁ הַזֶּה.
זָכְרֵנוּ יְיָ אֱלֹהֵינוּ בּוֹ לְטוֹבָה,
וּפָקְדֵנוּ בּוֹ לִבְרָכָה
וְהוֹשִׁיעֵנוּ בּוֹ לְחַיִּים.

| 1

וּבְנֵה יְרוּשָׁלַיִם עִיר הַקֹּדֶשׁ
בִּמְהֵרָה בְיָמֵינוּ.
בָּרוּךְ אַתָּה יְיָ,
בּוֹנֶה בְרַחֲמָיו יְרוּשָׁלָיִם. אָמֵן.

| 2

Our God and the God of our Fathers:
may the memory of us and our fathers
rise and come before You, reach You
and be accepted for our well-being, with
the memory of Jerusalem Your city, the
memory of Your people the whole
house of Israel, on this day of *Rosh
Ḥodesh*. Remember us, O Lord our God,
for our well-being; be mindful of us on
this day for blessing; save us for life.

O rebuild Jerusalem the Holy City
speedily in our days. Be blessed,
O Lord, who in mercy rebuilds
Jerusalem. Amen.

YA'ALEH VEYAVO: This prayer is also inserted in the *Tefillah* on *Rosh Ḥodesh* and
during festivals. It is a very old prayer, referred to in the Talmud (Babylonian
Talmud, *Berachot* 29b).

זִכְרוֹן יְרוּשָׁלַיִם — THE MEMORY OF JERUSALEM: The emphasis on the restoration of Jerusalem to its full Davidic glory is spelled out with even greater emphasis
in the daily version of the *Tefillah*, known as *Tefillat Shemoneh Esrei* ("the *Tefillah* of
eighteen benedictions"). In his commentary on the prayerbook, the English scholar
Israel Abrahams suggested that these Jerusalem prayers probably go back to
pre-Maccabean times "and originally referred not to the rebuilding of Jerusalem
but to its building, and to its continued enjoyment of the Divine Presence. After
the destruction (70 C.E.), the contents of the prayers were modified to refer to the
re-building."

On the references to the House of David, Israel Abrahams says: "The connec-
tion between the Davidic tradition and the coming of the Messianic age was
strengthened in the last century of the Temple's existence. There has been a break
in the Davidic line when the Hasmoneans—a Priestly house—assumed the throne,
and this change became intolerable when the Herodians usurped the royal
dignity."

וּבְנֵה יְרוּשָׁלַיִם — O REBUILD JERUSALEM: This blessing is in the version now
popular, and is not the version in the Saadya *siddur*.

1

2

בָּרוּךְ אַתָּה יְיָ, אֱלֹהֵינוּ מֶלֶךְ הָעוֹלָם, הָאֵל אָבִינוּ מַלְכֵּנוּ בּוֹרְאֵנוּ גּוֹאֲלֵנוּ,	1	Blessed is the Lord our God, king of the universe; God, our Father, our King, our Creator, our Redeemer.
הַמֶּלֶךְ הַטּוֹב וְהַמֵּטִיב אֲשֶׁר בְּכָל־יוֹם וָיוֹם הוּא מַרְבֶּה לְהֵיטִיב, וְהוּא יִגְמְלֵנוּ לָעַד חֵן חֶסֶד וְרֶוַח וְרַחֲמִים וְכָל טוֹב.	2	The King, Who is kind and deals kindly; Who every day offers more kindness to us, bestowing on us grace, lovingkindness, redemption, mercy and all good things.

1 אָבִינוּ מַלְכֵּנוּ — OUR FATHER, OUR KING: The calm confidence of this prayer, and its reference to God as King, brings to mind a famous poem by Solomon Ibn Gabirol (1021-1055), in which he expresses his faith in God by limiting his plea to the sustenance of this simple trust—"neither more nor less." The version given in the *Penguin Book of Hebrew Verse* (T. Carmi, Ed.) reads:

> God Almighty: You who listen to the wretched and grant their desire, how long will You remain far from me and hidden? Night and day I entreat You, I cry out with a confident heart. I shall always praise You, for Your love is never-ending. My King: I wait for You, I put my trust in You, like one who has dreamt an obscure dream and places his trust in the interpreter. All I ask is that You listen to my plea. This is my request, neither more not less."

2 הַטּוֹב וְהַמֵּטִיב — WHO IS KIND AND DEALS KINDLY: This blessing is known by these key words—*hatov vehametiv* (literally, "the Good One who does good"). The Babylonian Talmud (*Berachot* 48b) says that it was added to the three basic themes of the *Birkat Hamazon* after the Bar Kochba revolt ended with the fall of Betar (135 C.E.).

This first section of the blessing—it is Saadya's version, much shorter than the usual one—is said to have been instituted by the rabbis of Yavneh in gratitude for the miracle that the corpses of the unburied dead of the siege of Betar did not decay, and that permission was ultimately given for their burial. (The American scholar Louis Finkelstein says that there is evidence that this blessing was known before the fall of Betar, and that it may have originated soon after Hadrian became emperor in 117 C.E.)

On Shabbat:

הָרַחֲמָן הוּא יַנְחִילֵנוּ יוֹם שֶׁכֻּלוֹ
שַׁבָּת וּמְנוּחָה, לְחַיֵּי הָעוֹלָמִים.

May the All-merciful let us inherit
the day which shall be wholly a
Sabbath and rest in life
everlasting.

For Rosh Ḥodesh:

הָרַחֲמָן, הוּא יְחַדֵּשׁ עָלֵינוּ
אֶת־הַחֹדֶשׁ הַזֶּה לְטוֹבָה וְלִבְרָכָה.

May the All-merciful renew this month
for good and for blessing.

מִגְדּוֹל יְשׁוּעוֹת מַלְכּוֹ וְעוֹשֶׂה חֶסֶד לִמְשִׁיחוֹ, לְדָוִד וּלְזַרְעוֹ עַד עוֹלָם.	1

He is a tower of salvation to His
king, and shows
lovingkindness to David His
annointed and his seed forever.

עוֹשֶׂה שָׁלוֹם בִּמְרוֹמָיו, הוּא יַעֲשֶׂה שָׁלוֹם עָלֵינוּ וְעַל כָּל־יִשְׂרָאֵל, וְאִמְרוּ אָמֵן.	2

He who makes peace on high,
may He make peace for us and all
Israel, and say ye: Amen.

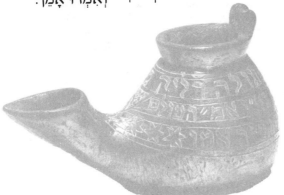

מִגְדּוֹל יְשׁוּעוֹת — A TOWER OF SALVATION: This verse is from II Samuel 22:51. [1]
It appears with a slight variant in Psalm 18:51, where the first word *migdol* is read
instead as *magdil,* to yield: "He gives great salvation." By custom, the Psalm's
version is used in the *Birkat Hamazon* on weekdays, and the version from Samuel on
Sabbath and Festivals.

עוֹשֶׂה שָׁלוֹם — HE WHO MAKES PEACE: We have seen that this sentence is used [2]
also to strike a note of peace at the end of the *Tefillah,* and at the end of the *Kaddish.*
It is a very popular verse, and is usually sung to conclude the recital of the *Birkat
Hamazon.*

The *Zemirot* ("songs") that we turn to
in the service are a good illustration of the
cheerfulness that has sustained
Jewish life perennially.

ZEMIROT

זְמִירוֹת

ZEMIROT: History is not recorded merely in archives. It emerges with equal—or greater—power in songs that surface among the people. The songs that have survived in the Bible—of Lamech, Moses, Miriam, Deborah, etc.—go back well over three thousand years. In post—Bible times, Jewish poets produced a vast literature of *zemirot* ("songs") in different styles. These songs remind one that Judaism is not just law and dogma but also a bubbling fountain of imagination and wit.

SOURCE AND STYLE: The Jews who pored over their study books day and night drew since earliest times on these beloved books to let their spirits soar poetically and playfully around the theme of being a Jew. Faith was the constant, but from that point on, the poets were inventive, allusive, rueful and jocular, all with a free rein. In phraseology, there were vast sources to draw on—the Bible, the Talmud, the Midrash, legend and folklore. One could be scholarly and pious, but that would never be enough. The lines had to be turned with skill; the rhythms had to be catchy; the audience had to accept it with delight.

Many poems, full of ingenious rhymes and rhythms, soon acquired a regular place in the daily service. But there were also lighthearted *zemirot* designed to be sung on Shabbat, particularly around the festive table. To call them "table hymns," as is sometimes done, can sound too ponderous. They are carols, though with a difference. However light their style, they always relate ultimately to the abiding feelings that history and faith generate among Jews.

POETRY AND MYSTICISM: The rich character of the *zemirot* emerges if one examines a *zemirah* like "Yom Zeh Leyisra'el" (see page 111). It seems at first merely a song of happiness—"This day is for Israel light and rejoicing, a Sabbath of rest." But we find that its author was Isaac Luria (1534–1572), the great scholar-mystic of Safed (Galilee), whose work in developing a system of Kabbalah had a profound influence on succeeding generations. This is typical of the bridge that exists between the sacred and the secular in Jewish life. Before his theoretical teaching became known, Luria had won fame as a poet. Gershom Scholem, the historian of Jewish mysticism, says of Luria's Sabbath songs: "Written in the language of the Zohar, they describe, in kabbalistic symbolism, the meaning of the Sabbath and the special relationship between man and Heaven on this day."

SHABBAT AS AN ENLARGEMENT OF LIFE: We are reminded, in one verse, that on Shabbat a Jew is infused with *neshamah yeteirah*—"an extra soul." This mystical thought is also the language of *zemirah*. How truly this thought captures our Shabbat joy!

1. YAH RIBON ALAM

יָהּ רִבּוֹן עָלַם וְעָלְמַיָּא,
אַנְתְּ הוּא מַלְכָּא מֶלֶךְ מַלְכַיָּא.
עוֹבַד גְּבוּרְתֵּךְ וְתִמְהַיָּא,
שְׁפַר קֳדָמָךְ לְהַחֲוָיָה.
יָהּ רִבּוֹן עָלַם . . .

Yah ribon alam ve'almayah,
ant hu malka melech malchaya.
Ovad gevurtech vetimhaya,
shefar kodamach lehaḥavaya.
Yah ribon alam . . .

שְׁבָחִין אֲסַדֵּר, צַפְרָא וְרַמְשָׁא,
לָךְ, אֱלָהָא קַדִּישָׁא דִּי בְרָא
כָל־נַפְשָׁא.
עִירִין קַדִּישִׁין וּבְנֵי אֱנָשָׁא,
חֵיוַת בָּרָא וְעוֹפֵי שְׁמַיָּא.
יָהּ רִבּוֹן עָלַם . . .

Shevaḥin asader tzafra veramsha,
lach, elaha kadisha di vera
chol nafsha.
Irin kadishin uvnei enasha,
ḥevat bara ve'ofei shemaya.
Yah ribon alam . . .

רַבְרְבִין עוֹבְדָיךְ, וְתַקִּיפִין,
מָכֵךְ רָמַיָּא וְזָקֵף כְּפִיפִין.
לוּ יְחֵא גְבַר שְׁנִין אַלְפִין,
לָא יֵעֹל גְּבוּרְתֵּךְ בְּחֻשְׁבְּנַיָּא.
יָהּ רִבּוֹן עָלַם . . .

Ravrevin ovdach, vetakifin,
machech ramaya vezakef kefifin.
Lu yeḥei gevar shenin alfin,
la ye'ol gevurtech beḥushbenaya.
Yah ribon alam . . .

God, Lord of the world and the universe: Thou art the king of kings.
The might of Thy work is wondrous: it is good to praise Thee.
God, Lord . . .
I will order Thy praises evening and morning:
holy God who createst all beings, sons of men,
beasts of the field, birds of the air.
God, Lord . . .
Great and mighty are Thy deeds, humbling the proud,
raising those who are bowed down. If we were to live a thousand years, it
would not be long enough to praise Your might.
God, Lord . . .

YAH RIBON: This Shabbat table song is in Aramaic, but was composed in the 16th
century by a kabbalist poet, Israel ben Moses Najara. (In the full version of five
verses, the name "Israel" is an acrostic spelled out by the first letter of each verse.)

2. YOM ZEH LEYISRA'EL

יוֹם זֶה לְיִשְׂרָאֵל אוֹרָה וְשִׂמְחָה,
שַׁבָּת מְנוּחָה.

Yom zeh leyisra'el ora vesimḥah,
shabbat menuḥah.

צִוִּיתָ פִּקּוּדִים בְּמַעֲמַד סִינַי,
שַׁבָּת וּמוֹעֲדִים לִשְׁמוֹר בְּכָל־שָׁנַי,
לַעֲרוֹךְ לְפָנַי מַשְׂאֵת וַאֲרוּחָה,
שַׁבָּת מְנוּחָה.
יוֹם זֶה . . .

Tzivita pikkudim bema'amad sinai,
shabbat umo'adim lishmor bechol shanai,
la'aroch lefanai mas'et va'aruḥah,
shabbat menuḥah.
Yom zeh . . .

חֶמְדַּת הַלְּבָבוֹת לְאֻמָּה שְׁבוּרָה,
לִנְפָשׁוֹת נִכְאָבוֹת נְשָׁמָה יְתֵרָה,
לְנֶפֶשׁ מְצֵרָה יָסִיר אֲנָחָה,
שַׁבָּת מְנוּחָה.
יוֹם זֶה . . .

Ḥemdat halevavot le'umah shevurah,
linfashot nich'avot neshamah yeterah,
lenefesh metzerah yasir anaḥah,
shabbat menuḥah.
Yom zeh . . .

קִדַּשְׁתָּ בֵּרַכְתָּ אוֹתוֹ מִכָּל־יָמִים,
בְּשֵׁשֶׁת כִּלִּיתָ מְלֶאכֶת עוֹלָמִים,
בּוֹ מָצְאוּ עֲגוּמִים הַשְׁקֵט וּבִטְחָה,
שַׁבָּת מְנוּחָה.
יוֹם זֶה . . .

Kiddashta berachta oto mikkol yamim,
besheshet killita melechet olamim,
bo matz'u agumim hashket uvit-ḥah,
shabbat menuḥah.
Yom zeh . . .

This day is for Israel light and rejoicing—
   a Sabbath of rest.
You bade us when we stood at Sinai to keep Sabbath and the Festivals,
   setting out a table full-laden—
   for the Sabbath of rest.
For a people in sorrow, the heart grows and overflows, banishing sadness
   and grief—
   on the Sabbath of rest.
When You finished the work of creation, You blessed this day above all
   others; the weary find peace and safety—
   on this day of rest.

YOM ZEH LEYISRA'EL: This was composed by Isaac Luria (1535-1573), as the acrostic spelled out by the first letter of each verse shows. Luria's *kabbalah* mysticism influenced all later generations; but he was also a poet, like his fellow kabbalists Israel Najara (author of *Yah Ribon*, p. 110) and Solomon Levi (author of *Lechah Dodi*, the song sung during the Sabbath eve service, p. 17).

3. YOM ZEH MECHUBAD

יוֹם זֶה מְכֻבָּד מִכָּל־יָמִים,
כִּי בוֹ שָׁבַת צוּר עוֹלָמִים.

Yom zeh mechubad mikkol yamim,
ki vo shavat tzur olamim.

שֵׁשֶׁת יָמִים תַּעֲשֶׂה מְלַאכְתֶּךָ,
וְיוֹם הַשְּׁבִיעִי לֵאלֹהֶיךָ,
שַׁבָּת לֹא תַעֲשֶׂה בוֹ מְלָאכָה,
כִּי כֹל עָשָׂה שֵׁשֶׁת יָמִים.
יוֹם זֶה . . .

Sheshet yamim ta'aseh melachtecha,
veyom hashevi'i lelohecha,
shabbat lo ta'aseh vo melacha,
ki chol asah sheshet yamim.

Yom zeh . . .

הַשָּׁמַיִם מְסַפְּרִים כְּבוֹדוֹ,
וְגַם הָאָרֶץ מָלְאָה חַסְדּוֹ,
רְאוּ כָל־אֵלֶּה עָשְׂתָה יָדוֹ,
כִּי הוּא הַצוּר פָּעֳלוֹ תָמִים.
יוֹם זֶה . . .

Hashamayim mesaprim kevodo,
vegam ha'aretz mal'ah ḥasdo,
re'u kol eleh asta yado,
ki hu hatzur po'olo tamim.

Yom zeh . . .

Supreme in honor is this day, when the Creator came to rest.
Six days we labor; the seventh we turn to God:
    Supreme in honor . . .
On Shabbat, no work for us, for everything was completed in six days . . .
    Supreme in honor . . .
The heavens and earth proclaim His glory; behold His wonder.
The Rock, His work is perfect.
    Supreme in honor . . .

---

4. VETAHER LIBBENU

וְטַהֵר לִבֵּנוּ לְעָבְדְּךָ בֶּאֱמֶת.
Vetaher libbenu le'ovdecha be'emet.

Purify our hearts to serve Thee in truth.

YOM ZEH MECHUBAD: The full version yields a name acrostic "Yisra'el Ha-ger," but nothing is know of him. Herbert Loewe says in *Medieval Hebrew Minstrelsy* (1926): "the metre, which is Provençal, is simple and common, and cannot be associated with any definite time."

VETAHER LIBBENU: This familiar phrase from the Shabbat *Tefillah* (see p. 59) is used as a chant or round.

5. MENUḤAH VESIMḤAH

מְנוּחָה וְשִׂמְחָה אוֹר לַיְּהוּדִים,
יוֹם שַׁבָּתוֹן יוֹם מַחֲמַדִּים.
שׁוֹמְרָיו וְזוֹכְרָיו הֵמָּה מְעִידִים,
כִּי לְשִׁשָּׁה כֹּל בְּרוּאִים וְעוֹמְדִים.

Menuḥah vesimḥah or layehudim,
yom shabbaton yom maḥamadim.
Shomrav vezochrav hemah me'idim,
ki leshishah kol beru'im ve'omdim.

שְׁמֵי שָׁמַיִם אֶרֶץ וְיַמִּים,
כָּל־צְבָא מָרוֹם גְּבוֹהִים וְרָמִים.
תַּנִּין וְאָדָם וְחַיַּת רְאֵמִים,
כִּי בְיָהּ יְיָ צוּר עוֹלָמִים.

Shemei shamayim eretz veyammim,
kol tzeva marom gevohim veramim.
Tanin ve'adam veḥayat re'emim,
ki veyah adonai tzur olamim.

Rest and joy. Sabbath is the day of delight for the Jew, saluting the miracle that all was created in six days—heaven and earth, the hosts on high and below, nature and man—all by the Rock of Creation.

6. ATTA EḤAD

אַתָּה אֶחָד וְשִׁמְךָ אֶחָד,
וּמִי כְּעַמְּךָ יִשְׂרָאֵל,
גּוֹי אֶחָד בָּאָרֶץ.
תִּפְאֶרֶת גְּדֻלָּה וַעֲטֶרֶת יְשׁוּעָה,
יוֹם מְנוּחָה וּקְדֻשָּׁה לְעַמְּךָ נָתָתָּ.
אַבְרָהָם יָגֵל, יִצְחָק יְרַנֵּן,
יַעֲקֹב וּבָנָיו יָנוּחוּ בוֹ.

Atta eḥad veshimcha eḥad,
umi ke'amcha yisra'el,
goi eḥad ba'aretz.
Tif'eret gedulah va'ateret yeshu'ah,
yom menuḥah ukdushah le'amcha natata.
Avraham yagel, yitz-ḥak yeranen,
ya'akov uvanav yanuḥu vo.

You are One, Your Name is One, and Your people Israel are one, garlanded with Your glory and salvation. You gave this holy day of rest to Your people—Abraham was glad, Isaac rejoiced, Jacob and his sons rested on it.

MENUḤAH VESIMḤAH: In the full version the acrostic name yields "Mosheh" (Moses). The meter is Provençal.

ATAH EḤAD: A jumble of familiar phrases, part of the *Tefillah* for the Shabbat afternoon (*minḥah*) service.

7. AN'IM ZEMIROT

אַנְעִים זְמִירוֹת וְשִׁירִים אֶאֱרוֹג,
כִּי אֵלֶיךָ נַפְשִׁי תַעֲרוֹג.
נַפְשִׁי חִמְדָה בְּצֵל יָדֶךָ,
לָדַעַת כָּל־רָז סוֹדֶךָ.
מִדֵּי דַבְּרִי בִּכְבוֹדֶךָ,
הוֹמֶה לִבִּי אֶל דּוֹדֶיךָ.
יֶעֱרַב־נָא שִׂיחִי עָלֶיךָ,
כִּי נַפְשִׁי תַעֲרוֹג אֵלֶיךָ.

An'im zemirot veshirim e'erog,
ki elecha nafshi ta'arog.
Nafshi ḥimdah betzel yadecha,
lada'at kol raz sodecha.
Middei dabri bichvodecha,
homeh libbi el dodecha.
Ye'erav na siḥi alecha,
ki nafshi ta'arog elecha.

Happily I sings my songs, for to Thee my spirit longs.
To trust in Thee is my delight, Thy mystery fills me day and night.
I hail Thy glory high above, my heart is moved to feel Thy love.
May I delight Thee with my songs, for to Thee my spirit longs.

8. ELIYAHU HANAVI

אֵלִיָּהוּ הַנָּבִיא, אֵלִיָּהוּ הַתִּשְׁבִּי,
אֵלִיָּהוּ הַגִּלְעָדִי
בִּמְהֵרָה יָבֹא אֵלֵינוּ
עִם מָשִׁיחַ בֶּן דָּוִד.

Eliyahu hanavi, eliyahu hatishbi,
eliyahu hagil'adi
bimherah yavo elenu
im mashiaḥ ben david.

Elijah the Prophet, Elijah the Tishbite, Elijah of Gilead—
May he come speedily, with the Messiah, son of David.

AN'IM ZEMIROT: The mystical ideas, expressed in mellifluous verse, have led some scholars to ascribe it to the main teacher of the German-Jewish mystics (Ḥasidei Ashkenaz) of the 12th century, Judah the Saint (Yehudah ben Samuel Heḥasid, c. 1150–1217).

ELIYAHU HANAVI: Familiar from the *Havdalah* service which concludes Shabbat and from the Pesaḥ *Haggadah,* this is a genuine folk song, with its own catchy tune.

9. OR ZARUA

אוֹר זָרֻעַ לַצַּדִּיק,
וּלְיִשְׁרֵי־לֵב שִׂמְחָה.

Or zarua latzadik,
ul-yishrei lev simḥah.

Light is sown for the righteous, and joy for the upright.

10. USH'AVTEM MAYIM

וּשְׁאַבְתֶּם־מַיִם בְּשָׂשׂוֹן
מִמַּעַיְנֵי הַיְשׁוּעָה.

Ush'avtem mayim besason
mima'ainei hai-shu'ah.

You shall draw water joyfully from the fountains of salvation.

11. ASHRENU MAH TOV ḤELKENU

אַשְׁרֵינוּ מַה־טוֹב חֶלְקֵנוּ,
וּמַה־נָּעִים גּוֹרָלֵנוּ,
וּמַה־יָּפָה יְרֻשָּׁתֵנוּ.

Ashrenu mah tov ḥelkenu,
umah na'im goralenu,
umah yafa yerushatenu.

O how happy, how good our lot! How beautiful our heritage!

12. VEKAREV PEZURENU

וְקָרֵב פְּזוּרֵינוּ מִבֵּין הַגּוֹיִם,
וּנְפוּצוֹתֵינוּ כַּנֵּס מִיַּרְכְּתֵי־אָרֶץ.

Vekarev pezurenu mibben hagoyim,
unfutzotenu kannes miyarketei aretz.

May our scattered ones come together from the corners of the earth.

OR ZARUA: The verse is Psalm 97:11, one of the *Kabbalat Shabbat* psalms.

USH'AVTEM MAYIM: A playful song out of the book of Isaiah (12:3), found in the prelude to the Saturday evening *Havdalah* service.

MAH TOV: Echoing the lyrical happiness of Psalm 133:1—"How good, how beautiful, for brethren to dwell together in unity."

VEKAREV PEZURENU: This is a familiar phrase from the *Tefillah* for festivals.

13. HINNEI MAH TOV

הִנֵּה מַה־טּוֹב וּמַה־נָּעִים
שֶׁבֶת אַחִים גַּם־יָחַד.

Hinnei mah tov umah na'im
shevet aḥim gam yaḥad.

How sweet and pleasing is brotherly love.

14. AMAR RABBI EL'AZAR

אָמַר רַבִּי אֶלְעָזָר,
אָמַר רַבִּי חֲנִינָא:
תַּלְמִידֵי חֲכָמִים
מַרְבִּים שָׁלוֹם בָּעוֹלָם.

Amar rabbi el'azar
amar rabbi ḥanina:
Talmidei ḥachamim
marbim shalom ba'olam.

Rabbi El'azar said, quoting Rabbi Ḥanina: "The students of the Torah increase peace in the world."

15. BARUCH ELOHENU

בָּרוּךְ אֱלֹהֵינוּ שֶׁבְּרָאָנוּ לִכְבוֹדוֹ,
וְהִבְדִּילָנוּ מִן הַתּוֹעִים,
וְנָתַן לָנוּ תּוֹרַת אֱמֶת,
וְחַיֵּי עוֹלָם נָטַע בְּתוֹכֵנוּ.

Baruch elohenu she-bera'anu lichvodo,
vehivdilanu min hato'im,
venatan lanu torat emet,
vehayei olam nata betochenu.

Blessed in God for whose glory we live. He gave us His Torah, and made our spirit immortal.

HINNEI MAH TOV: Psalm 133:1, quoted above on song 11.

AMAR RABBI EL'AZAR: This is a passage from the Talmud that appears in the traditional prayerbook to be read at the close of the service on Shabbat morning.

BARUCH ELOHENU: A jumble of familiar phrases, including some from the blessing one recites after being called up for the reading of the Torah.

16. HAḤAMAH MEROSH

הַחַמָּה מֵראשׁ הָאִילָנוֹת נִסְתַּלְּקָה,
בֹּאוּ וְנֵצֵא לִקְרַאת שַׁבָּת הַמַּלְכָּה.
הִנֵּה הִיא יוֹרֶדֶת, הַקְּדוֹשָׁה הַבְּרוּכָה,
וְעִמָּהּ מַלְאָכִים, צְבָא שָׁלוֹם וּמְנוּחָה.
בֹּאִי, בֹּאִי הַמַּלְכָּה!
בֹּאִי, בֹּאִי הַכַּלָּה!
שָׁלוֹם עֲלֵיכֶם מַלְאֲכֵי הַשָּׁלוֹם.

Haḥamah merosh ha'ilanot nistalkah,
bo'u venetzei likrat shabbat hamalkah.
Hinnei hi yoredet hakedoshah haberuchah,
ve'immah mal'achim tzeva shalom um-nuḥah.
Bo'i, bo'i hamalkah!
Bo'i, bo'i hakalah!
Shalom alechem mal'achei hashalom.

As the sun sets, let us go out to greet Queen Sabbath. She comes attended by angels of peace. Welcome, O Bride! Shalom, O angels of peace.

17. AMAR RABBI AKIVA

אָמַר רַבִּי עֲקִיבָא:
וְאָהַבְתָּ לְרֵעֲךָ כָּמוֹךָ —
זֶה כְּלָל גָּדוֹל בַּתּוֹרָה.

Amar rabbi akiva:
Ve'ahavta lere'acha kamocha—
zeh kelal gadol batorah.

Rabbi Akiva said: "'You shall love your neighbor as yourself.' This is the great principle of the Torah."

18. IM EIN ANI LI MI LI

אִם אֵין אֲנִי לִי מִי לִי?
וּכְשֶׁאֲנִי לְעַצְמִי מָה אֲנִי?
וְאִם לֹא עַכְשָׁו אֵימָתַי, אֵימָתַי?

Im ein ani li mi li?
Uch-she'ani le'atzmi mah ani?
Ve'im lo achshav ematai, ematai?

If I am not for myself, who will be for me?
Buf if I am for myself alone, what am I?
And if not now, when?

HAḤAMAH MEROSH: This is a short poem by Chaim Nachman Bialik.

AMAR RABBI AKIVA: His famed statement of the Golden Rule.

IM EIN ANI LI MI LI: An epigram—or paradox— coined by Hillel, appearing in *Pirkei Avot* (Ethics of the Fathers) 1:14.

19. ANI MA'AMIN

אֲנִי מַאֲמִין בֶּאֱמוּנָה שְׁלֵמָה
בְּבִיאַת הַמָּשִׁיחַ.
וְאַף עַל פִּי שֶׁיִּתְמַהְמֵהַּ,
עִם כָּל־זֶה אֲנִי מַאֲמִין,
עִם כָּל־זֶה אֲחַכֶּה־לּוֹ
בְּכָל־יוֹם שֶׁיָּבוֹא.

Ani ma'amin be'emunah shelemah
bevi'at hamashiaḥ.
Ve'af al pi she-yitma-meah,
im kol zeh ani ma'amin,
im kol zeh aḥakkeh lo
bechol yom sheyavo.

I believe with perfect faith in the Messiah's coming.
Though he tarry, I await every day, that he may come.

---

20. HATIKVAH

כָּל־עוֹד בַּלֵּבָב פְּנִימָה
נֶפֶשׁ יְהוּדִי הוֹמִיָּה,
וּלְפַאֲתֵי מִזְרָח קָדִימָה
עַיִן לְצִיּוֹן צוֹפִיָּה.
עוֹד לֹא אָבְדָה תִּקְוָתֵנוּ
הַתִּקְוָה שְׁנוֹת אַלְפַּיִם,
לִהְיוֹת עַם חָפְשִׁי בְּאַרְצֵנוּ
בְּאֶרֶץ צִיּוֹן וִירוּשָׁלָיִם.

Kol od balevav penimah
nefesh yehudi homiyah,
ulfa'atei mizraḥ kadimah
ayin letziyon tzofiyah.
Od lo avdah tikvatenu
hatikvah shenot alpayim,
lihyot am ḥofshi be'artzenu
be'eretz tziyon virushalayim.

So long as the Jewish heart is moved, the Jew will look East, to Zion.
Two thousand years and our hope is still not lost.
To be free in our own land, in Eretz Yisra'el, in Jerusalem.

ANI MA'AMIN: The philospher Maimonides (1135–1204) set out thirteen principles of belief, and these were popularized later in a credo Jews traditionally recited. This is the twelfth of the principles, adapted for chanting.

HATIKVAH: This is the Israel National Anthem, based on *Hatikvah* ("The Hope"), a poem written by Naphtali Herz Imber, probably in Jassy in 1878. In 1882, an immigrant to Palestine, Samuel Cohen, set it to a melody which he consciously based on a Moldavian folksong, echoes of which also appear in compositions by Dvorak. *Hatikvah* was formally declared the National Anthem at the 18th Zionist Congress in Prague, in 1933.